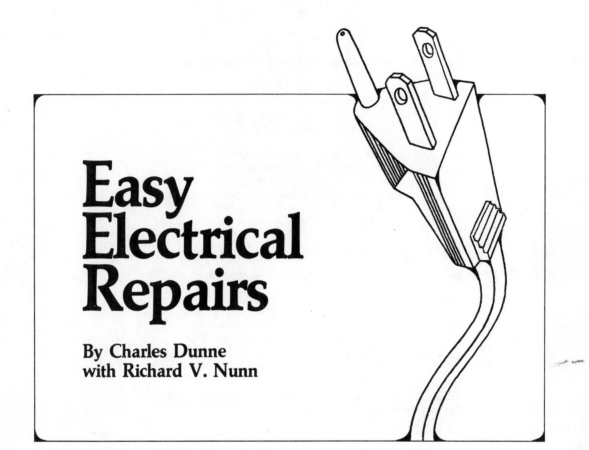

Easy Electrical Repairs

By Charles Dunne
with Richard V. Nunn

GALAHAD BOOKS · NEW YORK CITY

Published by arrangement with Oxmoor House, Inc.
ISBN: 0-88365-342-7

Copyright © 1976 by Oxmoor House, Inc.
Book Division of The Progressive Farmer Company
P.O. Box 2463, Birmingham, Alabama 35202.

Library of Congress Catalog Card Number: 75-32263

Manufactured in the United States of America

First Printing 1976

Easy Electrical Repairs

Editor: Grace Hodges
Schematic Drawings: John Anderson
Cover: Taylor Lewis

Contents

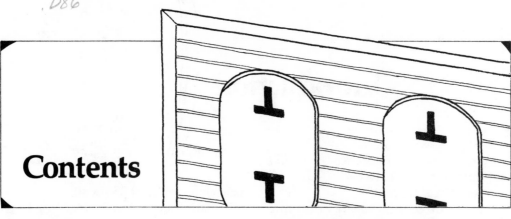

Introduction

Do you know the difference between a watt and a volt or between 50- and 60-cycle electrical current?

If not, you belong to the great majority of people who have only a passing understanding of electricity, although they use electricity hundreds of times a day. When an appliance groans and quits or a light switch goes out, most people start looking for help.

Easy Electrical Repairs has been written to relieve that helpless feeling. It is not intended to convert you to a full-fledged electrician, but it will give you a sound and basic understanding of what happens inside all those wires and electrical machines you depend upon so heavily.

Fortunately, the things you need to know about electricity aren't complicated. You will learn to make most of the simple electrical repairs around the house and to do so safely and correctly. You will still need to call the professional electrician from time to time, but only for the difficult work worthy of his attention.

There are several good reasons why you should understand electrical power. The first is for your own safety; when mishandled, electricity is dangerous. If you know how it works, then you will not make dangerous mistakes. Actually, electricity is no more dangerous than your automobile, which also can do great damage if you don't know how to use it or if you lose control of it.

The second reason for understanding electricity is to save yourself time and money. Most professionals are busy with major electrical work such as rewiring homes, and little repair jobs, like replacing a switch or installing a new wall outlet, are nuisances that must be worked into his schedule and for which you must pay well.

Still another reason for learning how to make your own electrical repairs is to avoid throwing away small appliances because they don't work. Maybe some of these cannot be repaired, but it is quite likely that many need only a cleaning of the contact points on the switch or a tightening of a loose wire. By knowing how to make simple repairs, you can keep a lot of your appliances working and save the cost of replacing them.

It might surprise you to know just how many electrical appliances, gadgets, and devices you use. Most people guess they have 20 or 25, but, in fact, the average home has more than 50, not counting the lights. To verify the figure, I counted the gadgets in my house and found 53, from electric blankets to hair curlers, and I didn't get around to the portable tools in my workshop or the outdoor devices such as the electric charcoal starter we keep in the garage.

Finally, by understanding electricity and the appliances we use, we can conserve energy while still enjoying electrical conveniences. To help you with this program, this book will teach you how to read your electric meter so that in less than five minutes a month you can keep track of just how much electric power you use. Fine, you say, but why not take the electric figures straight from the electric bill? Why bother to read the meter? The answer is simple. It is always a good idea to double-check every bill to see that a mistake hasn't been made. Errors creep into the very best systems, including the billing system used by your power company.

Now, on to the watts and volts.

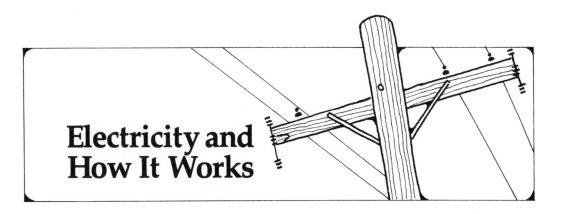

Electricity and How It Works

Electric power is a mighty servant. It does hundreds of jobs every day in the home and is a major contributor to the modern life-style; but it is also something of a mystery to most of us.

The following discussion of electrical terms will help remove some of this mystery and tell you how electricity works.

Current and voltage

The electric current flowing through the wires in your house is simply a steady stream of electrons which are developed by a generator at your power station and pushed through wires from the station to your home. The force, or pressure, that pushes this stream is called voltage, and the volt is a unit of measurement of this force.

Big generators at the power station produce tens and even hundreds of thousands of volts; this is enough electrical pressure to blast your home right off the street, if the current were to come directly from the generator to your fuse box.

What actually happens is that this current, under high pressure, is "pumped" into a network of wires through which it is distributed to thousands of homes and factories. At various points along this network, the current passes through transformers in power substations which act as local distributing centers. At each substation the voltage, or electrical pressure, is stepped down, and the current from the incoming line is divided and sent out over a number of smaller lines.

The great majority of the electric power generated in the United States is produced by burning fossil fuels, such as oil, coal, or gas in big power plants like this one.

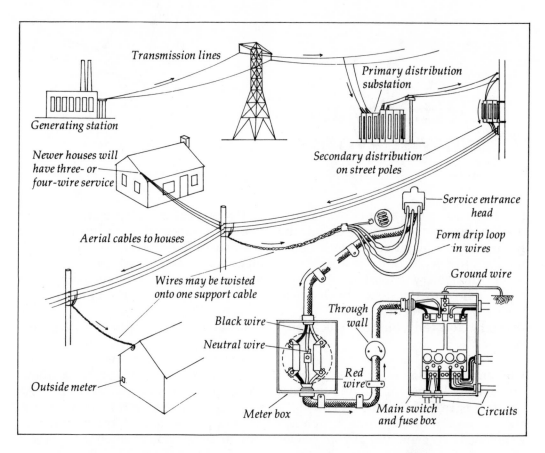

Transmission lines

Generating station

Primary distribution substation

Newer houses will have three- or four-wire service

Secondary distribution on street poles

Service entrance head

Aerial cables to houses

Form drip loop in wires

Ground wire

Wires may be twisted onto one support cable

Black wire

Neutral wire

Through wall

Red wire

Outside meter

Meter box

Main switch and fuse box

Circuits

By the time the current gets to the transformer that serves the houses on your block, the voltage has been reduced to perhaps 2300 and finally comes into your home as 230 volts.

We are all familiar with power failures, especially during electrical storms. In some places only the power on one street goes out; in other areas, whole square miles are blacked out. From the description of the power distribution network, you can see why this happens. When a transformer is hit, every power line beyond it in the network fails because it is no longer passing power along. Thus, if the transformer that serves your block is hit, only the few homes it serves will go black. But if a substation serving a whole neighborhood is hit, hundreds of homes will be blacked out until its transformer can be repaired.

The electric power coming to your house over this network of power lines is called power-line voltage, usually referred to as line voltage.

Keeping power in the line

It has been noted that voltage is the pressure pushing the current through electric wires. Most electric power companies maintain a nominal pressure of 115 volts in their lines, although this will vary from 110 to 121 volts. Your home's wiring and modern electrical appliances are made to function within this pressure range. If the pressure gets much higher than this, the wiring and appliances may be damaged; if it gets much lower, they lose their efficiency.

For the most part, power companies are able to control their line voltage quite well, but they face the problem of how people use electricity. Electricity must be put on the power lines as it is generated. This means that when the demand is low, some generators must be turned off; when the demand increases, more generators must be started.

At 3 a.m. power use is low. Between 5 and 6 a.m., the demand begins to increase rapidly and continues to increase

Nuclear-fueled generating plants are being built all over the country, but at present account for less than 3 percent of the electric power we use.

until it hits the day's peak around 2 p.m. The demand begins to taper off then but remains fairly high until midevening. Through all of this fluctuation the companies monitor demand and bring their generators on line as needed.

The greatest power use occurs in hot weather and is highest on the third day of a severe heat wave. This is the time when power-generating facilities are taxed to their utmost, with every piece of generating equipment working at full capacity; this is also the time when "brownouts" occur.

A brownout takes place when the power company has every generator in its system going full blast but still cannot generate enough power to meet the demand. The system can't keep 115 volts of electric pressure in the line, and the voltage slips down to 110, 105, 100, or lower. As the power gets lower, your lights get dimmer, the picture on your television set shrinks, and motor-driven appliances don't operate well.

Transformers on utility poles near your home are the last step-down units in the electric power distribution system. They reduce the power to the proper level to enter your home's electric system.

If the line voltage gets too low because of high demand, automatic safety devices cut off the power flow to prevent damage to the distribution system. Then you have a blackout.

Power companies go into action when a brownout appears imminent. They have agreements with industrial users who shut down their heavy equipment when the demand exceeds the supply. Appeals are sent out by radio, television, and newspapers asking all customers to cut down power use. Also, power companies are tied together in huge networks and can buy electric power from each other. When one company finds itself in trouble, it can buy power from other companies as far as 1,000 miles away, provided these companies aren't experiencing an excessive demand and have extra power to sell.

Real trouble occurs when a heat wave is widespread and no extra power is available or when big generators sud-

denly break down in the middle of a peak-demand period.

All of this means that a power company must have enough generating capacity to meet the highest anticipated demand of its customers, even though that peak demand may occur only once or twice a year, and it must have a reserve capacity to take care of breakdowns. With electric power demand increasing by 10 percent every year, most power companies have been racing to build generators to keep up with the peak demand; only a few have been able to get much ahead of it.

Ohms and heat

As already noted, voltage is the force that pushes the current through electrical wires. But wires tend to resist the passage of the current, and some metals resist more than others. Smaller wires resist more than big ones. This resistance is measured in a unit called an ohm (ōm). The more ohms of resistance a wire offers, the more voltage required to push the current through.

Whenever electricity is forced to overcome resistance, it develops heat; the greater the resistance, the greater the heat. This is an extremely useful attribute and makes possible both the electric light and electric heat.

In a light bulb there are tiny filaments made of metal that offer extremely high resistance to the passage of current. The resistance is so high that great heat is developed as the current passes through, causing the filament to turn white hot almost instantaneously. The glow of the white hot filament provides your electric light.

The same principle is employed in electric irons, toasters, and other devices that require heat to operate. The current is sent through wires of high resistance and causes them to become hot.

It takes many volts to push current through wires of high resistance. Only a few tiny filament wires are used in a light bulb, so the current demand is relatively small. But in electric irons and other appliances requiring a lot of heat, a large number of high-resistance elements are used. This explains why heating devices use so much more electric power than those devices that do not require heat.

Amperes and watts

If you could stand at one point on an electric wire and count the electrons that pass the point each second, you would be measuring the current's rate of flow. The unit of measurement for this is the ampere, usually referred to as an amp. (Don't try to memorize it, but you might like to know that one ampere is 6,280,000,000,000,000,000 electrons passing a given point in one second.)

The total power in your electrical system is a combination of current and voltage (the number of electrons moving per second and the amount of pressure pushing them), and it is measured in watts. You find the watt-age by multiplying the number of volts by the number of amps.

Thus, if your electric iron draws 10 amps and your line current is 115 volts, you multiply the two to discover that the power consumption of the iron is 1150 watts. The wattage figure represents the amount of energy consumed by the appliance in one second. By the same token, a 100-watt light bulb uses only .9 of an amp (100 watts divided by 115 volts = .9 amps). So, your electric iron uses about as much power as eleven 100-watt light bulbs.

You will find a metal plate or label on nearly every electrical appliance, which gives vital information about the appliance. It is important to know how to interpret this information. The plate on an electric dishwasher, for example, might read:

115 volts   12 amps   60 cycle   AC

The figure 115 volts means that the appliance was built to be operated with 115 volts of electric pressure or line voltage (but it will also give satisfactory service at about 10 percent above and below that figure).

The figure 12 amps tells you that the unit draws 12 amps of current when operating. Multiplying the volts (115) times the amps (12), you discover that it consumes 1380 watts. The reason for this heavy consumption is that heavy heating coils are used to dry the dishes after they are washed.

This figure of 1380 watts is extremely important to you, as you will see a bit later, when we look into the electrical circuits in your home. (*Note:* the watt-age figure is never exact but only reasonably close to the actual power consumption. This is because of the small variations in line voltage. When computing wattage, you can multiply by 110, 115, or 120 volts. The 115-volt figure is a good average.)

Electric cycles and AC/DC

To understand the figure 60 cycle, you must know how a generator works. This is complicated, and we won't get

The information plate on any electric appliance provides useful information. From this plate, you learn that this saw was built to operate on 115 volts, can be operated at any number of cycles from 25 to 60 hertz, which means it can be used in Europe, and draws 10 amps when operating. You also see that it has the Underwriters' Laboratory approval mark.

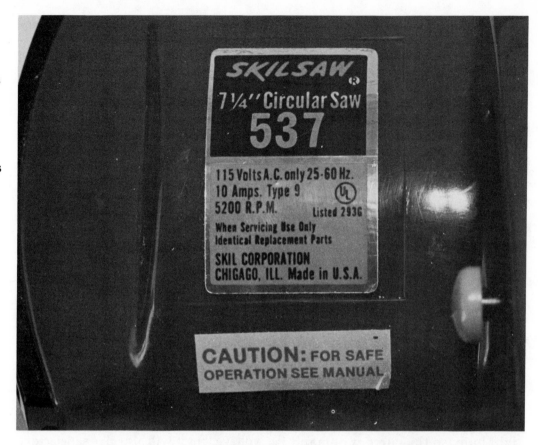

into a long explanation but just say that a generator looks like an electrical motor with a spinning center that revolves inside a stationary outside piece. Both the center and outside piece are wrapped in thousands of feet of fine copper wire. As the center, or rotor, turns, electric power is generated.

All electricity has polarity. You've seen evidence of this on your automobile battery where one post is marked positive (+) and the other negative (−). Electric current flows from the negative to the positive posts in a battery system, passing through the appliance or device on the way. (If you connected the posts directly, without running the current through an appliance, you would create a short circuit. The flow of current in a battery is always the same, from negative to positive, and is called direct current. All batteries supply direct current.

An electric generator of the type mentioned above and used by power companies, however, develops a different kind of current called alternating current, or AC. It does this because, as the rotor in the generator turns, it is alternately positive through one half of its rotation and negative through the other half. Thus, it produces alternating pulses of positive and negative current to send out through the power line.

The cycle number on an appliance information plate refers to the number of these alternating pulses sent out by the generator each second. American and Canadian power companies have standardized on 60 cycles per second. In Europe, however, the standard is 50 cycles. Many American-built appliances can't be operated on European current, although some are built to operate on either 50 or 60 cycles.

Obviously, as long as you are in the United States or Canada using appliances made in either country, you don't need to worry about cycles. If you

All batteries, from automobile storage units to the tiny cells in a transistor radio, supply direct current.

plan to take an appliance to Europe, read the information plate to see whether or not it will operate on 50 cycles. If not, you can buy a plug-in converter to take with you.

The word "cycle" is presently being phased out of the language of electricity and is being replaced by the word "hertz." So when you see "60 hertz" on an appliance information plate, it means the same as "60 cycle."

As for alternating and direct current, just keep in mind that all line voltage in your house is alternating current, and all power from any size battery is direct current.

Appliances designed for AC cannot be operated on DC current. That is, you can't use battery power to run a machine designed for line current, and you can't plug a device designed for DC battery power into a wall inlet. If you do, you will damage it severely.

You can, of course, buy converters for small battery-operated devices such as tape recorders. You plug the converter into a wall outlet and into the unit. The converter does two things. First, it converts the AC line current to DC current; then it steps down the line current from 115 volts to the voltage required by the unit, usually 6 or 9 volts.

When buying a converter, get one for the unit you want to power. The voltage output of most converters is preset and cannot be adjusted. If your tape recorder, for example, requires 6 volts, a converter which supplies 9 volts should not be used with it.

Some portable radios are built to operate on either batteries or line current. These have converters built right into them, and you must push a switch to go from one to the other. Also, some appliances are made to operate on both AC and DC power. The information plates on these will be marked AC/DC. The reason for this is that electric line voltage is DC in a few places in the world. Electric power in the United States and Canada started out as direct current but long ago was converted to alternating current.

Equipment designed for battery operation was made to run on direct current. It cannot be plugged into an AC line unless an adapter is used. The adaptor changes the AC current to DC and reduces it from normal line voltage to the power needed by the unit, which is usually 6 to 9 volts.

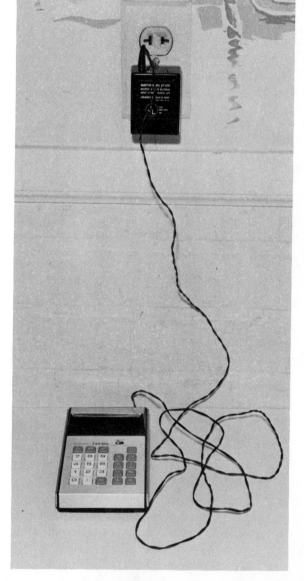

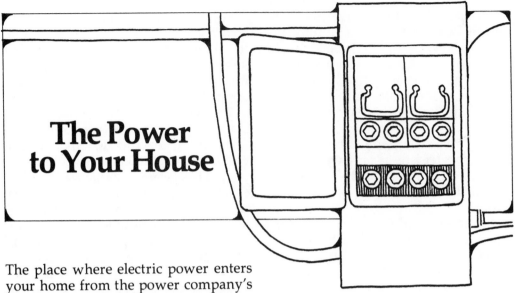

The Power to Your House

The place where electric power enters your home from the power company's line is called the service entrance. If you go outside and look at your service entry, you will see either two or three wires coming from a nearby utility pole to the entrance head, which is located 10 feet or more above ground level on the side of your house. The wires come down the side of your house inside a pipe to the electric meter. Just below the meter, they go through the wall of the house into the main service panel, or fuse box, located inside the house.

In some communities, power lines are buried underground instead of being carried on utility poles. In this case, your service wires will come up out of the ground near your home and run to the meter.

This home has three-wire electrical service. The center wire of the three is neutral, while the other two each carry 115 volts.

If it appears that you have two-wire service, look a second time. In some installations, you can see three separate wires. In others, two of the wires are twisted around each other, while the third wire is separate. In two-wire installations, you will see two separate single wires.

The power company is responsible for the service line as far as the meter. Once the line leaves the meter, it becomes the responsibility of the homeowner.

If there are only two single wires from the utility pole to your home, you are receiving only 115-volt power. This means that you probably don't have as much electricity as you need in this day of electrical appliances and heavy power use. You should consider having your home rewired, both for safety and convenience. When you do, the power company will provide three-wire service, and your electrician will install a new main service box and new circuits throughout the house to take advantage of the additional power.

If your house has three entrance wires, you now have 115-230 volt power. This means that you have enough power to operate an adequate number of circuits and to use a large number of appliances. It also means that you can have a 230-volt circuit for an electric stove or large air conditioner.

In a three-wire circuit, there is one white wire, called the neutral wire, and two black (or another color other than white or green) "hot" wires. Each black wire is used with the white wire to provide 115 volts, so you have two 115-volt service lines. In addition, the two black lines can be joined in your main service box to provide the 230-volt range and heavy appliance circuit.

Main service center

The service line enters your home and goes directly to the main service center, or fuse box. If you look into this box, you will see that the incoming service wires are connected first to two main fuses located near the top of the box. The chief purpose of these fuses is to protect your home in the event of a large surge of power in the line, such as might occur if lightning strikes the power line or transformer.

You will also see that a heavy wire leads away from the fuses and into a conduit. If you follow this conduit, you'll find that it leads to a cold-water pipe. This is the wire by which your electrical system is grounded. To ground the system, a solid connection to earth must be made, and the cold-water pipe is the best and most convenient method of making this contact.

These main fuses usually are marked **MAIN** and **RANGE.** The fuse marked **MAIN** protects all the 115-volt circuits, and when it is blown (which is very seldom), there is no power in any 115-volt circuit in the house. The fuse marked **RANGE** protects the 230-volt circuits. When both fuses are removed, no electricity can enter the wires in your home.

In some installations these main fuses may be located in a small service box alongside the service center. It is a good idea to become familiar with your system and to know how to turn off the power in the event of an emergency. The time to do this is now, when no emergency exists.

> *When resetting a fuse or circuit breaker, turn off all appliances first, reset, then turn appliances on one at a time. Otherwise, the sudden power demand will blow the fuse or trip the circuit breaker again.*

Below the main fuses in the service box, you will see either two neat rows of circuit breakers or a collection of screw-in fuses. Each circuit breaker has a small switch. When there is a problem in the circuit the breaker protects, this switch automatically flips open, disconnecting the circuit. After you solve the problem, reset the circuit breaker by pushing the switch closed once more.

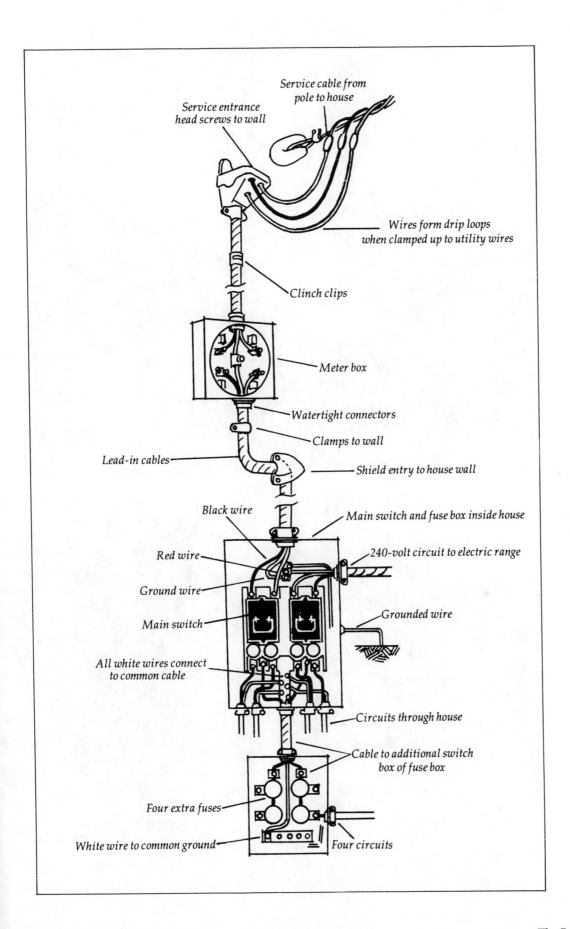

Service cable from pole to house

Service entrance head screws to wall

Wires form drip loops when clamped up to utility wires

Clinch clips

Meter box

Watertight connectors

Clamps to wall

Lead-in cables

Shield entry to house wall

Black wire

Main switch and fuse box inside house

Red wire

240-volt circuit to electric range

Ground wire

Main switch

Grounded wire

All white wires connect to common cable

Circuits through house

Cable to additional switch box of fuse box

Four extra fuses

White wire to common ground

Four circuits

Most three-wire service is brought to the home through twisted wires, such as these. To find out whether you have two- or three-wire service, count the number of wires actually entering the service entry head.

Right:
Power enters the home at the main service box. This box has 8 fuses, showing that there are 8 separate circuits in the home. The two black squares with the wire handles at the top of the box are the main fuses for the entire system.

Far right:
The inside of a fuse box looks like this when the protective plate is removed. The black wire, attached to the screw beneath each fuse, is the "hot" wire for the circuit protected by that fuse. The very thick white wire near the bottom of the box is the system's grounding wire, which is fastened to a cold-water pipe not far from the fuse box.

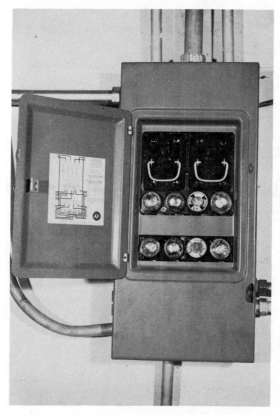

This home is protected by circuit breakers instead of fuses. The advantage is that there are no fuses to replace. To put a circuit back in operation, after it has been shut off because of a short circuit, you need only to reset the circuit-breaker switch.

Sometimes the main fuse is located in a separate box beside the main box containing the circuit fuses or circuit breakers. This home has 200-amp service, and each of these cartridge fuses is rated at 100 amps. You can turn off all the power by pulling down on the handle at the right side of the box.

If there is trouble in a line protected by a screw-in fuse, a tiny metal band inside the fuse melts and, in so doing, disconnects the circuit. Once the fuse has been blown, it must be removed and replaced by an undamaged fuse of the same value, usually 15 or 20 amps.

In boxes with circuit breakers, the main fuses may also be circuit breakers that operate in the same manner as the smaller breakers in the box. More likely, you will see two blocks with small handles on them. To remove these fuses, you pull the handles, and lift out the blocks. Looking at the back of each block, you'll see two cartridge fuses — fuses that are several inches long and look like shotgun cartridges.

In some older service boxes, these cartridge fuses may not be in blocks but may be inserted between brass clips in the service box. **If you ever remove cartridge fuses of this type, use extreme care, and wear rubber gloves, since it is easy to accidentally touch exposed metal and receive a fatal shock.**

Safety precautions

Even if you are very familiar with electricity, always approach the main service box with a great deal of respect. Don't ever take chances when working in or near it, and always know exactly what you intend to do before opening it. Don't poke around in it with your hands or with tools.

Here are some safety precautions that could save your life. Pay attention to them.

1. When entering the main service box for any reason, don't stand on

Right:
To shut off the power completely, pull the main fuses. Rubber gloves are an excellent safety precaution when working in the main service box; they protect you if you should accidentally brush against an exposed wire.

Far right:
Pull out the main fuses, and turn them around; you find that each has two cartridge fuses inside. The chief function of these fuses is to protect your home against surges in the power line, such as would occur if lightning were to strike the power line or a transformer. They also provide a quick and handy method of shutting off all power.

a wet floor. If the basement floor is anything but bone dry, put down a couple of short 2 x 4s to serve as a dry platform.

2. The service box is constructed so that a panel covers all exposed wires and circuit connections. Always make sure that this panel is in place and securely screwed down before changing a fuse. It will protect you from accidentally touching a bare wire.

3. Never touch any bare wire in the service box.

4. For absolute safety when working around the box wear rubber-soled shoes and thick rubber gloves.

5. Learn how to turn off all the power. In some cases, you may have to pull the main fuse blocks; in others, there is a handle at the side of the service box which, when pulled down, shuts off all current. For safety's sake, turn off the current by either of these methods, even when changing a fuse. Changing a fuse isn't a dangerous operation, but you could accidentally touch a hot wire as you work. If the current has been turned off, nothing will happen to you. If it is on, you may receive a severe shock.

How much power do you have?

You remember that power is measured in watts, and wattage is found by multiplying volts times amperes. The average 115-volt power line provides 30 amps of current, and two of these in the three-wire service provide your home with 60-amp service. Sixty amps are considered a bare minimum for a small home and inadequate for

Far left:
Keep a pair of rubber gloves hanging near the main service box, and put them on every time you change a fuse. It takes only a moment, and it could prevent a serious accident.

Left:
Never touch the main service box or anything in it when the basement floor is wet or even damp. To make sure you aren't grounded through a damp floor, stand on a couple of dry boards. When working on electricity anywhere in the basement or outside the house, it is a good idea to wear rubber-sole shoes.

larger homes and for those with many appliances.

The service now considered minimal is three-wire, 115-230 volt service providing 100 amps of current. If you have an electric range, electric clothes dryer, electric heat, or an electric hot-water heater, you should have 150- or 200-amp service.

To discover how many amps you are receiving, check your main fuses by pulling the block marked **MAIN**. You'll find two cartridge fuses inside, one for each hot wire. Look at the ratings marked on the sides of these fuses. If each is a 30-amp fuse, then you have 60-amp service. If each is 50 amps, then you have 100-amp service.

The importance of knowing how many amps you receive is that by knowing both volts and amps, you can compute the total number of watts you have available for use in your home.

Here is a handy chart to use.

*3-wire 60 amp service provides 13,800 watts
3-wire 100 amp service provides 23,000 watts
3-wire 150 amp service provides 34,500 watts
3-wire 200 amp service provides 46,000 watts
*60-amp service × (2) 115 volt circuits = 13,800 watts

At no time should the current used in your home exceed the number of watts available. While some of these numbers look pretty big, it doesn't take long to build up the number of watts being used, if you have appliances that are heavy current users. An electric water heater, for example, may use as much as 4500 watts, and an electric range as much as 16,000 watts. Add another 8000 watts for an electric clothes dryer, and you have a total power demand of 28,500 watts just for these appliances alone.

Power Used By Appliances*

Appliance	Watts	Amps
Air conditioner, window	750	6.5
	1000	8.7
	1300	11.3
Blanket, electric (single)	250	2.1
(dual)	450	3.9
Clock	3	.02
Fluorescent light, one tube	50	.4
Fan, attic	400	3.4
Fan, table	75	.65
Fan, vent: kitchen, bath	70	.6
Furnace, gas or oil	800	6.9
Hair dryer	300	2.6
Heater, room	600	5.2
Heating pad	60	.5
Hi-fi stereo	300	2.6
Humidifier	500	4.3
Light bulbs	as marked	½ amp per 60 watts
Radio	75	.65
Shaver	10	.08
Sump pump	300	2.6
Sun lamp	275	2.4
Television, 18" B & W	300	2.6
Television, 18" Color	350	3.0
Vacuum cleaner	400	3.5

Power Used By Appliances* *(Continued)*

Appliance	Watts	Amps
Kitchen and Laundry		
Blender	250	2.1
Can opener	100	.85
Coffee maker	600	5.2
Dishwasher	1800	15.6
Freezer	600	5.2
Frying pan	1400	12.0
Fryer, deep	1400	12.0
Garbage disposal (small)	500	4.3
(large)	900	7.8
Grill	1300	11.3
Iron, hand	1100	9.5
Ironer (mangle)	1650	14.3
Mixer, food	150	1.3
Oven, microwave	650	5.6
Refrigerator	250	2.1
Rotisserie	1400	12.0
Roaster	1400	12.0
Stove, small electric	1650	14.3
Toaster	1100	9.5
Washer, clothes	900	7.8
Waffle iron	1100	9.5
Tools		
Drill press	800	6.95
Drill, portable (small)	200	1.7
(heavy-duty)	400	3.4
Saw, circular	1150	10.0
Saw, radial	1500	13.0
Saw, saber	400	3.4
Soldering iron	100	.85
Heavy-duty, needing		
230-volt circuits		
Air conditioning, central	5000	43.5
Range	8000	69.5
	16,000	139
Washer/Electric Dryer	5200	45.2
Water Heater (small)	2500	21.7
(large)	4000	34.7

*The chart shows the average number of watts consumed by a given appliance. This is a help in making a general estimate of the loads you are putting on your circuits. However, the consumption varies from model to model, so eventually you should compute the actual consumption of the appliances in your home. Remember the formulae (using 115-volt circuit): watts divided by volts equals amps; amps times volts equal watts.

Individual circuits

The electric power in your house is divided into separate circuits. Each circuit begins at its own fuse in the main service box.

There are three types of household circuits: general purpose, appliance, and special purpose.

General-purpose circuits

A general-purpose circuit serves house lights and wall outlets throughout the house, except for those wall outlets in appliance circuits in the kitchen and laundry room. For many years electricians installed one general-purpose circuit for each 375-square feet of floor space and protected each circuit with a 15-amp fuse.

More recently general-purpose circuits have been increased to serve 500 square feet of floor space and have been protected by 20-amp fuses. (*Note:* If your circuits were designed for 15-amp fuses, you must continue to use them. You can't change the capacity of a circuit simply by changing the fuse; changing the circuit's capacity also involves changing the size of the wire used in the circuit. Putting a 20-amp fuse in a 15-amp circuit reduces the protection the fuse provides and can lead to an electri- cal fire if you overload the circuit.)

To determine how many general-purpose circuits your house should have, divide the number of square feet of living area by 375. Thus, if you have 2000 square feet of living area, you should have at least 5, and preferably 6, general-purpose circuits. Two thousand divided by 375 is 5.3). If you now have fewer than 5 circuits, you should consider adding more.

If, for example, you now have 4 circuits, you have adequate wiring for 1500 square feet. By adding one 20-amp circuit, which serves 500 square feet, you make your wiring adequate for 2000 square feet.

You can put as many outlets as you want in any circuit, placing them where they are most convenient. The rule in good wiring is to have a wall outlet for each 12 running feet of wall. The wall outlets should be convenient to the location of your furniture.

Keep in mind that every circuit has a watt capacity, which you learn by multiplying volts times amps. A 15-amp circuit thus has a capacity of 1725 watts (15 × 115 = 1725). A 20-amp circuit has a capacity of 2300 watts. This means that you can use lights and appliances on these circuits up to the total

Consider adding some new wall outlets, if some of your electrical outlets look like this. Otherwise, you might be overloading the circuit by drawing more electric power than it was designed to provide. This causes the wires in the circuit to overheat and creates a fire hazard.

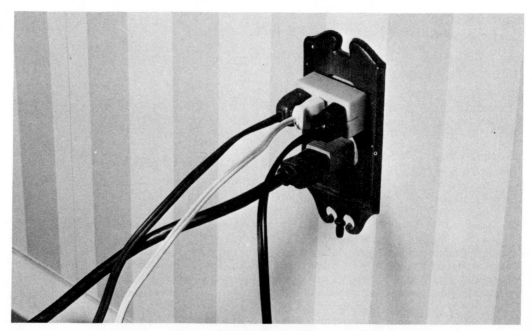

capacity, but no more.

Suppose, for example, that your family room is on one 15-amp circuit, which has a 1725-watt capacity. You'd like to iron clothes here while you watch television. Your 18-inch color TV set uses 350 watts. Your iron uses 1100 watts. The room is lighted by two 100-watt bulbs. Is it safe to put these lights and appliances on this one circuit?

The answer is yes. When you add up the wattage, 1100 + 350 + 100 + 100, the total is 1650 watts. However, if the kids come home from school and want to plug in an electric corn popper, rated at 300 watts, you have to say no. This appliance would raise the total to 1950 watts and overload the circuit.

Appliance circuits

In addition to general-purpose circuits, your home should have special appliance circuits. The National Electrical Code requires at least two 20-amp, grounded-type circuits for kitchen and laundry appliances.

An appliance circuit must be separate from any lighting circuits; all of the wall outlets on it must be of the three-prong type so that the appliances are grounded when in use. As a rule of thumb, you should plan one wall outlet for each 4 feet of kitchen-counter space.

The same rules used to compute the watt capacity of general-purpose circuits apply to appliance circuits. Each appliance circuit has a capacity of 2300 watts which should not be exceeded. Kitchen appliances use more watts than you might suspect, so you should watch carefully to see that you don't overload these circuits.

For example, when preparing breakfast, you might use the coffee maker (600 watts); the toaster (1100 watts); and the juice squeezer (150 watts). This totals 1850 watts. If your refrigerator is plugged into this line, add another 250 watts. The total is now 2100 watts, which is safe. If, however, you plug the electric frying pan in to cook bacon, you add another 1400 watts, and seriously overload the circuit.

Because using appliances in combinations, such as the one just mentioned, is not unusual today, the wall outlets in your kitchen should be on two circuits; then you can divide the electrical load between them.

Special-purpose circuits

Appliances that are heavy users of current are often given their own fused circuits. Your furnace, dishwasher, or

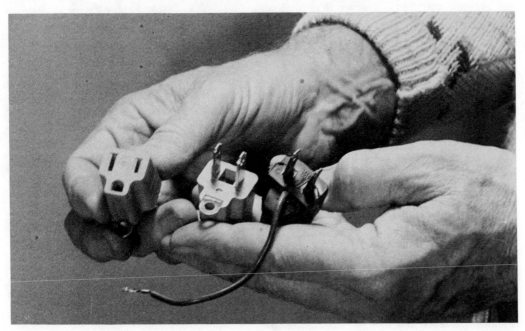

Converter plugs, which enable you to use an appliance with a three-pronged grounding plug in a standard two-prong outlet, can create a hazardous situation, unless you make the ground connection. One type of plug has a grounding wire, another has a metal grounding tab. Both fit under the screw in the center of the wall plate on the outlet and take only a moment to connect.

garbage disposer, may be on its own circuit, which is usually a 20-amp circuit that is separately fused. In other words, the line from the main service box may lead to a small fuse box near the appliance. The fuse provides additional protection.

It is wise to be aware of any special-purpose circuits and know where the fuses are located; otherwise, you can spend a lot of time trying to find out why you can't get an appliance to work when the problem is simply a blown fuse in the special fuse box.

Heavy-duty appliances such as electric ranges, hot-water heaters, clothes dryers, and central air-conditioners require 230-volt circuits and usually are on individual circuits of their own. You must not plug a 115-volt appliance into a 230-volt circuit, and to prevent your doing this, 230-volt appliances have a special three-prong plug that fits into a special three-prong outlet. You cannot insert a standard plug into this outlet.

Map your present circuits

It is a good idea to make an electrical map of your home, especially if you

Right:
Heavy duty equipment, such as this whole-house air-conditioner, usually is put on a single circuit and separately fused. The fuse box for this unit is located on the wall, at right.

Far right:
Inside the fuse box of a large air-conditioning unit you find a fuse similar to the main fuse in your main service box. There are two cartridge fuses in the back of this box.

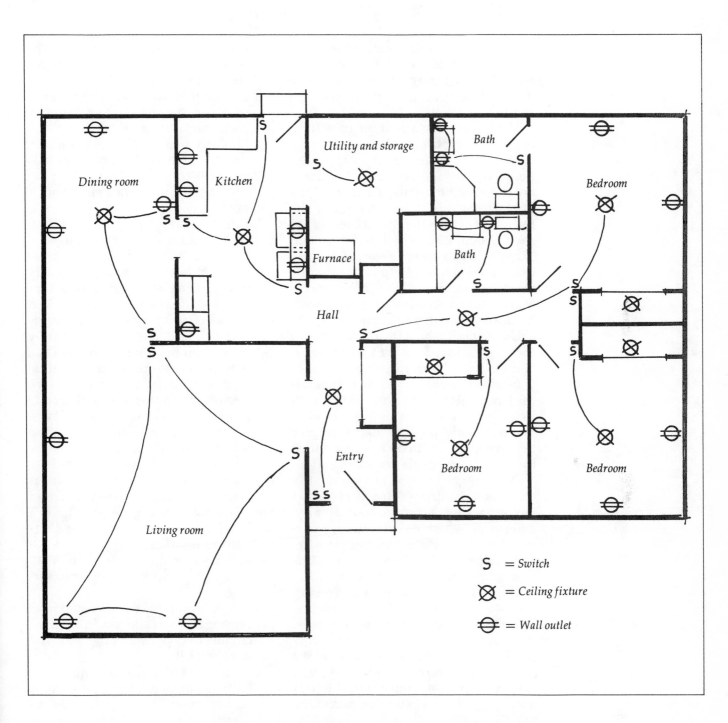

Dining room

Kitchen

Utility and storage

Bath

Bedroom

Furnace

Bath

Hall

Entry

Bedroom

Bedroom

Living room

S = Switch

⊗ = Ceiling fixture

⊖ = Wall outlet

have moved into it recently or have never attempted to identify the individual circuits. You can use the map to determine possible circuit overloading and to aid in planning new circuits.

Begin by making a floor plan sketch of each floor of the house; include the basement and garage. Now indicate the location of every ceiling fixture, wall outlet, and wall switch by using sym-

bols you can recognize: a circle for ceiling fixtures; an S inside a square for switches; two circles inside a small rectangle for wall outlets. (There are recognized electrical symbols for these things, but the map is for your own use, so use symbols that have meaning for you.)

Next make a sketch of your main service box showing the fuses or circuit breakers and assigning a number to each, i.e., Circuit No. 1, Circuit No. 2, etc. Make the map easier to read by using a different colored pencil for each circuit.

Now comes the important job of finding out which circuit serves each switch, fixture, and wall outlet in the house. Circuits for fixtures and switches are the easiest to locate. Turn on all the lights, then, one at a time, remove the fuse or switch off the circuit breaker for each circuit; note which lights go out. (Remember to observe the safety precautions when working in or near the main service box. *Don't take chances.*) Mark the circuit number next to each fixture and switch on your map.

Use a small table lamp as a tester in the wall outlets. Turn off Circuit No. 1, and plug the lamp into those sockets you believe should be on that circuit. If the lamp fails to light when you plug it in, mark that circuit number next to that wall outlet on your map. Continue the procedure until you have identified the circuit number of every wall outlet.

Don't forget to draw in and identify each special-purpose circuit as well as any separate fuse boxes. And, finally, determine which circuits supply current to your doorbells, intercom system, and kitchen and bathroom ventilating fans, and enter these on the map.

The results of this mapping may surprise you. Usually, lights, switches, and outlets for each circuit are grouped close together in the house. But if someone has added outlets or switches, or adjusted the circuits in any way, you may find one lone outlet on the first floor coupled to a circuit that serves the second floor.

Analyze the circuits

Sit down and study the map. Compute the watt capacity of each circuit, and note this next to the fuse or circuit breaker on the chart you have made of the main service box. Ask yourself the following questions:

- Do I have enough general-purpose circuits? (You need a 15-amp circuit for each 375 square feet of living space, or a 20-amp circuit for each 500 square feet.)
- Do I have at least two appliance circuits serving the kitchen, laundry room, and dining room?
- Has any heavy-duty equipment, such as dishwasher, garbage disposer, etc., been installed that should be on a separate circuit but is not?
- Could I make living more convenient by adding new wall outlets?
- In our daily use of appliances are we accidentally and habitually overloading any circuit? (Perhaps you use the toaster, coffee maker, and electric frying pan on the same circuit. This doesn't necessarily mean you need new circuits. You may be able to correct the situation by dividing the use between two circuits. To do this, you will need to install a new wall outlet or two, which is a much simpler job than adding a new circuit.)

The objective of this analysis is to determine whether or not your house is adequately wired. You may discover any of the following:

- Your service from the power company is insufficient. If you have 60-amp service, for example, you may find you need 100- or 150-amp service.
- Although you have sufficient power coming in, you need to add or adjust circuits to take care of the way you use electricity.
- Your present arrangement of circuits is adequate, but you need to add more wall outlets for convenience.
- Your present system is adequate. If you find this to be true, take a moment to consider the future. Will this system also be adequate later on? Do you plan to add more appliances? How would such an addition affect your system?

When you finish the analysis, you should know any inadequacies of your home's electrical system.

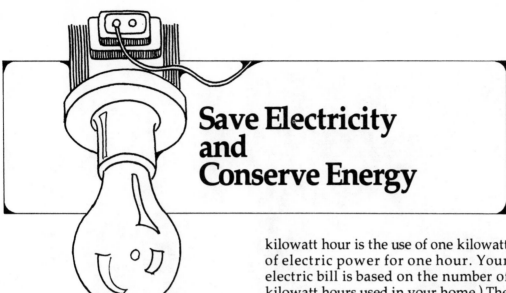

Save Electricity and Conserve Energy

Most of us could save quite a bit of money each year and help to conserve the nation's vital energy resources by cutting down on our use of electric power. We can make this savings without having to give up any of the comfort and convenience supplied by our electric appliances. All we need to do is carefully monitor our use of electric power, and cut out the waste. Electric power is handy and wonderfully easy to use; unfortunately, it is also easy to waste.

In the United States, we now use about 1.7 million megawatts of electric power a year. (A megawatt is a million watts.) About 80 percent of this power is produced by generators driven by oil, gas, and coal, and about 5 percent presently comes from nuclear-powered generators. The remaining 15 percent comes from hydroelectric generators that are driven by water pent up behind river dams.

You won't be able to see the oil or gas saved when you cut down on the use of electric power, but you can see a real result in your electric bill; it will get smaller.

Save on lighting

To see how electric power savings can be translated into real dollars in your pocket, here is an example. If you burn a 100-watt light bulb steadily for one year, you would use 876 kilowatt hours. (A kilowatt hour is 1000 watts. A kilowatt hour is the use of one kilowatt of electric power for one hour. Your electric bill is based on the number of kilowatt hours used in your home.) The rate for electric power varies from area to area, but if you paid 3¢ per kilowatt hour, which is a low average rate, it would cost you $26.28 for the year's use of this light bulb. However, if the next year you replaced it with a 60-watt bulb, you'd use only 525 kilowatt hours, and your bill at the end of the year would be only $15.55, a savings of $10.51.

Use as much light as you need, but don't overlight. Don't use a 100-watt bulb where a 60 will do. Don't light a small hallway with a 60-watt bulb, if a 40-watt bulb permits you to safely see where you are going.

A big waste of electricity is leaving lights on in an empty room, unless it is necessary for security reasons. A single hour of such waste doesn't cost much, but, as shown, over a year these single hours build up to an appreciable total.

Save on big power consumers

Check your use of those appliances that consume a lot of electric power, such as air-conditioning equipment and appliances that produce heat. Can you use them a little less than you now do?

A medium-size window air-conditioner, for example, costs about $3^{1}/2$¢ an hour to use. If you can use it for one hour less each day, your monthly electric bill will drop by a dollar.

Do you keep the electric coffee maker plugged in all day? Coffee makers use from 600 to 1000 watts, depending on the unit; so you can figure it costs you

Right:
When left plugged in all day, the coffee pot can be an expensive luxury, costing as much as $9.00 a month in electricity. For every hour you keep it unplugged, you can save from 2¢ to 3$\frac{1}{2}$¢.

Far right:
Air-conditioners, even the smaller window units, are big power users. During the warm months, if you cut your use by only an hour a day, you can save a considerable amount of energy and money. Latest models have been designed to use less power than older units; some deliver the same cooling for as much as one-third less electricity.

Don't pull a plug from a wall outlet by tugging on the wire. The correct way is to pull the plug, not the wire. Pulling the wire can loosen the connections inside the plug and cause a short circuit.

The Cost of Electric Energy*

Electric Appliance	Annual Energy Use	Annual Cost
Air-conditioner	2,000 kwh	$60.00
Can opener	1 kwh	.03
Clock	17 kwh	.51
Clothes dryer	1,200 kwh	36.00
Coffee maker	100 kwh	3.00
Dishwasher	350 kwh	10.50
Electric blanket	150 kwh	4.50
Fan, furnace	480 kwh	14.40
Fluorescent light	260 kwh	7.80
Food freezer (16 cu. ft.)	1,200 kwh	36.00
Food mixer	10 kwh	.30
Food waste disposer	30 kwh	.90
Frying pan	240 kwh	7.20
Hair dryer	15 kwh	.45
Hot plate	100 kwh	3.00
Iron	150 kwh	4.50
Lighting	2,000 kwh	60.00
Radio	20 kwh	.60
Radio-phonograph	40 kwh	1.20
Range	1,500 kwh	45.00
Refrigerator (12 cu. ft.)	750 kwh	22.50
Sewing machine	10 kwh	.30
Shaver	1 kwh	.03
Television (black and white)	400 kwh	12.00
Television (color)	550 kwh	16.50
Toaster	40 kwh	1.20
Vacuum cleaner	45 kwh	1.35
Washer (clothes)	100 kwh	3.00
Water heater (electric)	4,200 kwh	126.00

*These figures from the *Reader's Digest 1975 Almanac* show the average annual energy use and annual cost of home appliances in a typical American home. The cost is based on a charge by utilities of 3¢ per kilowatt hour. In most communities the cost will be several cents higher, as the cost of energy rises annually.

between 2¢ and 3¹/2¢ per hour for warm coffee. If you unplug it for a couple of hours each day, you will reduce your bill by perhaps $2.00 a month.

Read your meter

Probably the best way to force yourself to save electric power is to become conscious of just exactly how much power you use each month. Get a little notebook, and write in it the number of kilowatt hours you use every month. Just seeing the numbers written down will motivate you to try an economy program.

There are two ways to find out how many kilowatt hours you use. One is to take the figure from your electric bill. The other is to read the meter yourself. In many communities, electric bills are issued every two months, which is a long time to wait for information when you are on an energy-saving program.

The electric meter is glass covered and located outside the house near the service entry. If you look at it, you'll see either four or five small dials, like clock faces, with pointers. Two of these rotate in a clockwise direction, and two counterclockwise. If your meter has five dials, three will move clockwise. These dials record the number of kilowatt hours of electric power that enter your home.

You can easily read these dials yourself. Begin with the first dial on the left. Record the number that the little pointer has just passed. If the pointer is between 7 and 8, then write down 7. Do the same reading for the second and third dials.

The fourth dial (or fifth, if your meter has five dials) is read a little differently. On this one you write down the number the pointer is approaching; if the pointer is between 3 and 4, you record 4.

Suppose you decide to check your power use closely for a few weeks, and decide to take a meter reading each Saturday morning. On the first Satur-day, take a reading, and record it. On the second Saturday, take another reading, and subtract the first reading from the second. The difference will be the number of kilowatt hours you used during the week.

Power companies charge customers on several different rate scales. Large industrial power users, for example, pay at a different rate than homeowners. The rate code is noted on your bill. This does not indicate what you pay for power but refers to the rate scale by which you are charged. To find out exactly what you pay per kilowatt hour, call the customer service desk at your power company. The rate usually is based on a descending scale, so that the more power you use, the lower the price per kilowatt hour.

You can find the average cost of a kilowatt hour without calling the power company simply by using the figures on your electric bill. Divide the number of kilowatt hours shown on the bill into the dollar amount shown. If you used 495 kilowatt hours, and your bill is for $19.54, you are paying an average of 3.9¢ per kilowatt hour.

All electric meters have either four or five small clock faces that keep track of the number of kilowatt hours used by the customer. If the pointer is between numbers, record the lower number on the first three (or four) dials and the higher number on the fourth (or fifth) dial. This meter shows a reading of 0762.

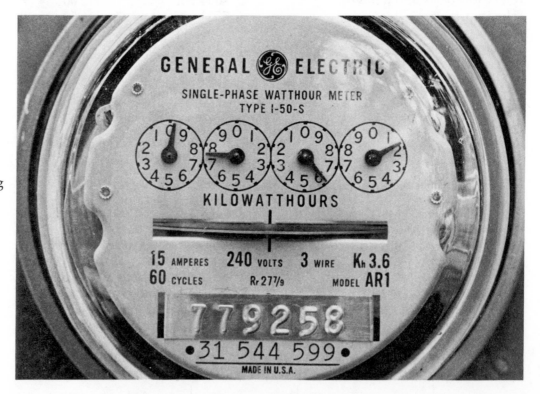

Electrical Safety

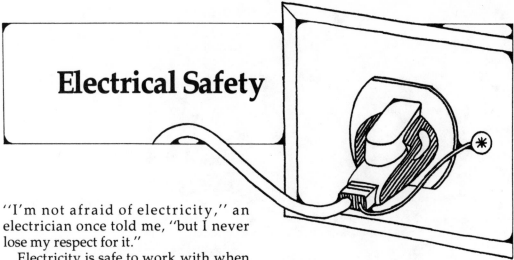

"I'm not afraid of electricity," an electrician once told me, "but I never lose my respect for it."

Electricity is safe to work with when you pay attention to what you are doing but very dangerous when you are careless. Safety is simply a matter of knowing how to be careful.

Electric shock

Nearly everyone has experienced an electrical shock and found it unpleasant. A severe shock interferes with heart and breathing action and can be fatal. It is the current (amperage, not voltage) that is dangerous, and a shock of 1/10 of an ampere can kill.

When you touch live wires, your body becomes a conductor, and the amount of current passing through your body depends on the voltage driving it and on the resistance your body offers. If any part of your body is wet, the electrical resistance is lowered, and a greater current flows through it. This is why it is so dangerous to have wet hands and wet feet when you are working with electricity. A shock, which would no more than sting you when you are dry, can kill you when water lowers your electrical resistance. For safety's sake, you want to avoid being shocked, but especially avoid being shocked when wet or even damp from perspiration.

Safeguards

There are several safety features built into your electrical system: the insulation on all wires, the fuses or circuit breakers, and the grounding of major electrical appliances.

Insulation

To be effective, insulation must cover the wire completely. If it is cracked or broken or worn, it may permit an electrical leak. Always replace wires that appear to be deteriorating; they are a source of danger and trouble.

Fuses and circuit breakers

When there has been a short circuit, the fuses blow or circuit breakers trip disconnecting a circuit and shutting off the power. Breaking the circuit prevents overheating of the wires, a major cause of electrical fires. If you find the same fuses blowing repeatedly, don't install a larger capacity fuse. The blown fuses indicate an overloaded circuit, and a larger fuse will permit the wires in the circuit to overheat. Correct the situation by reducing the load on the circuit.

Grounding of appliances

Electric current always follows the path of least resistance. Loose connections, deteriorating wire, or moisture inside an appliance can cause a short circuit. The stray current from the short looks for a place to go. If the appliance has a three-prong plug, it is grounded through the round extra prong. If the appliance is not grounded, and you touch it, you get a stiff shock. If you happen to have wet hands or to be in contact with a grounded item, such as a stove or water pipe, the shock can be fatal.

Avoid electrical accidents around your house by replacing all wiring that shows signs of deterioration. The cord on this iron should have been replaced a long time ago. Check old extension cords, too, especially if they are stored for long periods between use. The insulation may have become brittle, causing it to develop tiny cracks when you use it.

When a short circuit causes a circuit breaker to flip to the "off" position, resetting it takes no more than a push of the switch. However, if the trouble in the circuit hasn't been taken care of, the switch will again flip to "off." Therefore, when a fuse or circuit breaker blows, always correct the problem before putting in a new fuse or flipping the breaker to "on."

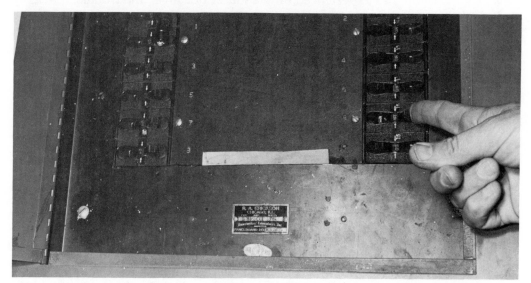

If you don't have wall receptacles that will take three-pronged plugs, you can use a converter plug. There is a short wire on the side of this plug that must be attached to the wall outlet by means of the screw that holds the outlet's faceplate in position. The wire must be installed under this screw. If the wire isn't screwed in place, the appliance isn't grounded, and it can give you a serious shock if a short develops.

It is better to install grounded recep-tacles in those wall outlets where you use grounded appliances than to use converter plugs. You will learn how to do this simple job in Chapter Seven, "Working on Household Circuits."

System grounding

The National Electrical Code requires a third wire in all home electrical circuits for the grounding of electrical equipment. The third wire is connected to the metal box in which each switch

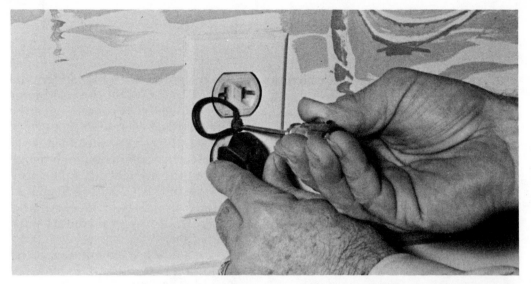

Connecting the ground wire to the screw in the center of a wall-outlet plate takes only a moment with a small screwdriver. Any grounded appliance will operate without being grounded through this screw, but you lose valuable protection against shock unless the connection is made.

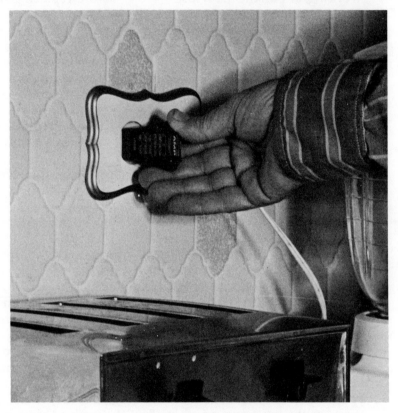

Are the grounded circuits in your house (the ones with three-prong receptacles) *actually grounded?* Perhaps someone tinkering with the electric circuits unknowingly broke the continuous ground. An electrician can test your circuits for you, or you can buy an inexpensive plastic tester, and make your own test. When you plug it into a grounded outlet, little neon lights indicate whether the circuit is grounded or not, and whether the "hot" and neutral wires are correctly installed.

or receptacle is mounted. In this way, there is a continuous ground line the length of the circuit and back to the main service box.

If your home has been wired using either rigid or thin-wall conduit tubing, the conduit itself serves as the ground conductor in the system. In this case, a wire runs from a grounding screw on the receptacle to a screw in the side of the box to make a sure ground connection.

Your entire system should have this grounding continuity, if your local electrical code requires it. It must have this continuity in those circuits used as appliance circuits. Unfortunately, you have no way of knowing whether an amateur has tampered with this grounding continuity or not when making additions or repairs to the original electrical system. To be sure, you can have an electrician check the system. He does this with a device called a "megger," an instrument designed to test the condition of a grounding electrode. Or you can buy an inexpensive three-prong tester and check your own system.

Safety rules

To assure safety when you are working with electrical circuits or appliances, follow these suggestions:

- Never work with a live electric wire. Always cut off the current before starting work; take out the circuit fuse, turn off the circuit breaker on the circuit on which you are working, or pull the main fuse.
- Never work on anything electrical near water. Don't stand on a damp or wet floor. Use a couple of 2 x 4s as a dry platform. Don't have wet hands or feet.
- Before beginning any electrical work, remove all rings, wristwatches, bracelets, and other metal items that might accidentally contact a live wire.
- Though they seem clumsy, heavy rubber gloves offer good protection when you work around the main service box.
- If your basement floods, be careful. Don't step into the water because it may be in contact with live electricity through one of the appliances, and contact with the water could electrocute you. Later, when the water has subsided, but the floor is still wet or damp, don't attempt to work on the appliances. And even after the floor is dry, flooded appliances may still have water in them, or the parts and wires inside may be wet. (Have the appliance repair service come and check your machines.) Water makes electricity very dangerous.
- Wear shoes with rubber rather than leather soles when making electrical repairs.
- Be cautious when using a metal ladder, particularly when working outside. Never let the ladder contact the incoming power line. And remember that when the ladder is in contact with the ground, and you

are in contact with the ladder, you are grounded. What can be a minor shock under other conditions can be fatal in this case.

If standing on the metal ladder to use electric tools, a drill or a hedge trimmer, for example, make sure the feet of the ladder are insulated from contact with the earth and avoid flesh-to-metal contact with the ladder.

- When a fuse has blown, correct the condition that caused it to blow before replacing the fuse. If the cause was too many appliances on the circuit, disconnect some. If you suspect a short in an appliance, unplug that appliance. Unplug the main fuse before taking out the blown fuse, and be sure you are standing on an absolutely dry floor. To be safe, put a dry board under your feet; then replace the blown fuse.

Ground fault interrupter

You have many appliances that do not have the three-pronged grounding plug, such as the toaster, mixer, iron, coffee maker, and can opener. These appliances can develop current leaks and internal short circuits just as do heavy duty units, particularly after long service. The short can be caused by a loose wire, or wires with cracked and worn insulation.

When this happens, the bare wire contacts the appliance frame or case and may create a dangerous situation. However, if the unit is grounded through a three-pronged grounding plug, the current will return through the ground and blow a fuse, warning you that something is wrong.

Since these appliances aren't grounded, they can continue to operate in normal fashion. If you touch the unit, however, you'll receive a shock. And if you are grounded because you are touching a pipe or a gas stove, or if you have wet hands, the shock can be fatal.

Recently a device called a ground fault interrupter has been developed to protect you in this situation. There are

Far left:
Metal ladders are fine conductors of electricity, especially when they are grounded by being in contact with the earth. If you are in contact with the metal, you also are grounded. If there is a short circuit in the tool you are using while on the ladder, or if you accidentally cut through the power cord, the resulting shock can be fatal. Safety suggestions: wear rubber-sole shoes; don't let your skin touch the metal, especially if you are wet or perspiring; use the appliance on a grounded circuit; insulate the feet of the ladder from the earth by using a board or sheet of heavy plastic.

Left:
Be extremely careful when using a metal ladder in the vicinity of your electrical service entrance. Don't permit the ladder to contact the wires, and don't climb the ladder near the wires. Stay alert to the danger when painting or making repairs near these wires.

Protect yourself by insulating the feet of metal ladders from contact with the earth. This ladder has no-slip feet, which also serve as insulation. However, your weight may cause the ladder to dig in and make contact in spite of these feet. Don't rely on them alone.

two types of ground fault interrupters. One is an adapter, which plugs into a wall outlet, and into which you can plug any ungrounded appliance. The other is a fixed unit combined with a circuit breaker, which is installed permanently in main service boxes—one for each circuit.

Using a GFI, you will receive a very slight shock in the event of a short circuit in the appliance you are using. But a solid state circuit in the GFI very quickly senses the problem and shuts off the line current. The action is so quick that you feel only a momentary and very slight sting, which is good, because it warns you not to use the appliance again until it has been repaired.

The GFI was originally developed for use in electrical circuits around swimming pools, where current leaks from the pump or water purification system create an electrical hazard. It has special application in all wet areas, such as laundry rooms, but is equally useful with any ungrounded appliance, such as a hair dryer.

National Electrical Code

The National Electrical Code is compiled in a 536-page book of recommendations for safe methods of installation and specifications for the construction of electrical equipment. Published by the National Fire Protective Association, it was first issued in 1897 and is revised regularly to include the latest safety developments.

The NEC is only a set of recommendations and not a law. However, most communities use it as a basis for local electrical codes that are the law. Any electrical work performed in a community must conform to the specifications of the code. Even though most codes are based on the NEC, they vary considerably from community to community.

Before starting any major electrical work on your home's system, read a copy of your local electrical code. Most communities have printed copies available in the office of the building inspec-

tor. Write for an abridged version of the NEC called "One- and Two-Family Residential Occupancy Electrical Code" by sending $2.00 to the National Fire Protective Association, 470 Atlantic Avenue, Boston, Massachusetts, 02210.

You must, in most communities, obtain a permit to do major electrical work. When the work has been completed, it must be inspected by the building inspector or a designated master electrician, who certifies that the work was done in accordance with the code.

No permit is required for simple jobs like replacing switches and wall outlets. Keep in mind that the code doesn't prevent you from doing the work yourself on larger projects; it simply requires that you do the work in a specified manner and that the work be inspected and passed by a master electrician.

Homeowners who do their own electrical work sometimes ignore the requirements of the local code, including the need for a permit and inspection. However, if they ever have a fire of electrical origin, the fire insurance company may cancel coverage because of this uninspected electrical work.

Underwriters' Laboratories

The Underwriters' Laboratories was established for the purpose of testing electrical products submitted to it by manufacturers. If a product passes the UL tests, it may then carry the UL label, which tells you that certain materials and design standards have been met.

UL approval is not a guarantee of top quality. You may find several switches at your hardware store at different price and quality levels, all with the UL label. All of these switches are safe to use, will work as you expect, and conform to the specifications on the label. The more expensive ones may last longer, be easier to install, or have additional features. But the least expensive is safe to buy, if you choose to do so.

For reasons of safety, it is a good idea to buy only those electrical components that carry the UL label.

The conduit coming from the lower left of this main service box carries the system's ground wire. You can see where it is clamped to the cold-water pipe between the floor joists (upper left-hand corner). Every system is grounded either by means of a connection similar to this or through a connection to a long metal rod driven into the ground.

To assure that your electric ground is continuous, even if the water meter should be taken out for replacement, a heavy grounding wire is clamped to the water pipe on both sides of the meter.

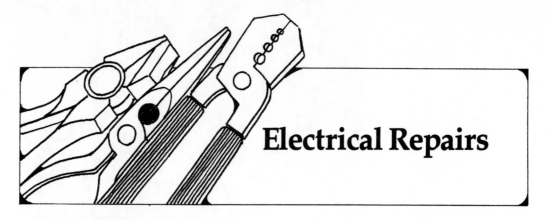

Electrical Repairs

Should you attempt to make electrical repairs yourself, or should you have them done by a professional? The answer depends on you.

To begin with, working with your electrical system (rewiring, adding new amperage or new circuits) is a precise business. Each layout, each connection must be handled in the precise way laid down by your electrical code. Experience has shown that these methods produce the safest systems.

There is no reason why you can't learn these precise methods and do the complete job yourself. But when installing a main service box or rewiring a house, there is no room for guesswork or for improvised methods. Even if you get the system to work with these methods, you may have built a potential fire into it.

So the answer for major overhauling of your electrical system is to do it yourself, if you can do it right. Otherwise, call an electrician. The smaller jobs also have to be done precisely; but these are uncomplicated procedures which you can learn quickly.

This chapter and the succeeding ones will help you to identify your electrical problems, show which ones you can solve, and demonstrate how to do so safely and correctly.

Faulty wiring system

How do you know when your house wiring system needs help? The system itself will tell you; here are some signs to watch for:

- **Fuses blow frequently.** The circuit is overloaded. The cure is to add another circuit, and divide appliances between circuits.

- **Lights seem dimmer than they should but get brighter when appliances are turned off.** You need to add power to the system. If you have 100-amp service, you probably need 150 or 200 amps.

- **Air-conditioner isn't cooling as it should.** A separate circuit for the unit may provide the power it needs. If not, increase service power by going to 150 or 200 amps.

- **Lights flicker frequently** (especially as appliances are turned on). An increase in amperage is needed.

- **You are using many extension cords.** Increase number of wall outlets.

- **You use cube taps** (those plug-in sockets that permit you to use several appliances from one wall outlet). Increase the number of wall outlets, and check to see if a new circuit is needed in the area where these appliances are used.

- **Sometimes a switch doesn't work when you flip it.** Replace it; the switch is worn out.

- **Appliance plug and cord are very hot.** These are indicators of an overloaded circuit. Add a new circuit or change appliance to a different existing circuit.

- **Automatic features of appliances seem sticky.** (The toast doesn't always pop, and the washer sometimes skips a cycle). The probable cause is low amperage, and you are using more appliances than your present power supply can handle. Call the power company to discuss increasing your home's amperage.

- **You get a slight shock when you**

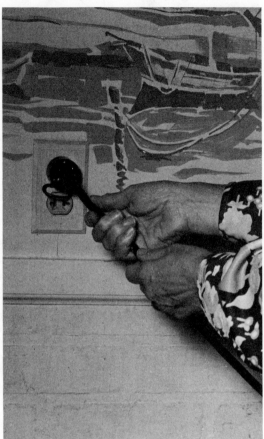

Far left:
If you must flip a switch several times before it works, it should be replaced. The working parts are worn and are not making proper contact.

Left:
Feel the plug and power cord of any appliance. If it feels unusually hot, it may be an indication of an overloaded circuit. Check the other appliances plugged into the circuit at the same time, and add the total wattage of these appliances. A 15-amp circuit is overloaded when the wattage exceeds 1725, a 20-amp circuit, when the wattage exceeds 2300.

touch the outside of an appliance. Don't use the unit until it has been repaired, because there is a short inside. Check for the source of the short, and repair it.

The above list distinguishes five basic problems. The biggest one, and the most costly to fix, is that your house has outgrown its electrical system. You may have 3-wire 60-amp or 100-amp service, but you now operate so many appliances that you need 150- or 200-amp service. This is a common condition even in homes that aren't very old.

Unless your power company is having severe expansion problems, it can supply increased amperage; you can find out by calling the customer service department. But in order to handle the increased amperage, your system will have to be revamped, starting at the main service entrance. Existing circuits can remain, but new ones should be added.

The second biggest problem is that your use of appliances doesn't conform to the layout of your system. For example, over the years you have added more and more kitchen appliances and now need two or three kitchen circuits, but you have only one. Your system may have enough power, but that power isn't distributed so that you can use it. This means adding new circuits, which is a substantial wiring job beginning at the main service entry box.

Two other problems are less severe. Old and worn switches and wall outlets aren't functioning properly. These can easily be replaced. If there are not enough wall outlets or if they are inconveniently placed, add new outlets to the existing system.

The final problem doesn't relate to the house system but to faulty appliances, which have developed internal short circuits. These, as a rule, can be repaired.

The handiest tools to have when doing repair work on your electrical circuitry are a power drill and jigsaw. You could use an auger-and-bit and keyhole saw instead, but power tools make the job go much faster. You also need fish tape and a plug-in tester. The fish tape is a thin, flexible wire used to pull wire through conduit and through long runs in walls, and you can rent one of the containers. The plug-in tester will tell you whether or not your grounded circuits are actually grounded.

Only a few hand tools are needed for electrical repair work: regular and needle-nose pliers, wire cutter, an assortment of screwdrivers, hacksaw, wire stripper, single-edge razor blade (which is good for cutting through insulation), two-wire tester (which, when inserted into a wall outlet, gives you a quick indication of whether the circuit has power or not), and plastic electrical tape.

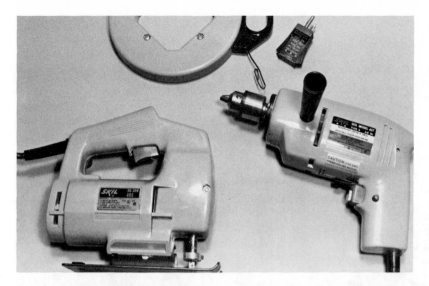

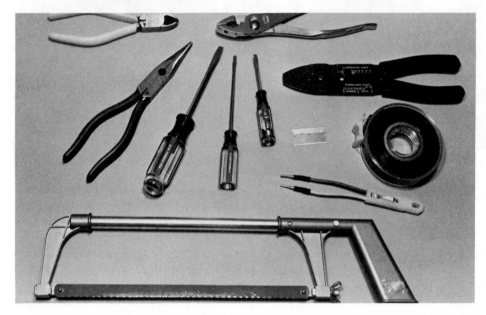

Tools

You won't need a lot of specialized tools for most electrical work, and you probably have all but a few in your toolbox right now.

Two power tools, a good electric drill and a saber saw, will come in handy. However, you can use a hand-powered keyhole saw in place of the saber saw.

You can use a wire clipper and several pliers including standard, small standard, and needlenose. Add a hacksaw for cutting armored cable, a builder's hammer, and a set of insulated screwdrivers. You'll need very small screwdrivers for appliance repairs, and two or three larger ones for typical circuit repairs.

A conduit cutter and a conduit bender can be rented if you need them to work on thin-wall conduit. You'll also use a wrench to tighten the conduit connections, although this can be done with pliers.

The handiest tool of all, and one which will save your time and temper, is a wire stripper. This is an inexpensive tool and a good one to own even if you do no more than occasionally rewire a lamp.

Materials

You won't need much in the way of installation materials: a roll of plastic electrical tape and a handful of solderless connectors in various sizes, plus the wire, switches, outlets, and fixtures you add to the system.

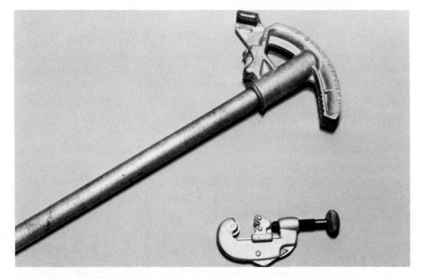

Thin-wall conduit is a lightweight tube through which electrical wires are carried. When installing thin-wall conduit, you will need a bender and a cutter, which you can rent.

Every electrical connection must be made inside a protective junction box, according to both the National Electric Code and most local codes. There is a junction box made for every imaginable application. The easiest way to get the right one is to tell your dealer where you intend to use it, and he can make the selection. Some boxes are shallow, some deep. You can buy them to fit one, two, or three switches or outlets to be used on every type of wall, such as plaster, plasterboard, etc. All have precut openings on all sides; to use an opening, simply punch out the tab with a screwdriver.

Wiring devices

Modern electrical materials are easy to use. All the parts are standardized and designed to work together. You don't have to worry about whether one manufacturer's wall outlet box takes another maker's wall outlet. All fittings are made in standard sizes.

The materials needed are conduit or armored cable, mounting boxes, connectors for attaching conduit to boxes, and mounting hardware necessary for ceiling fixtures.

Keep in mind that the main purpose of wiring devices is to protect the wires that carry the current and to shield you from that current.

Visualize a typical circuit in your system. It begins in the main entry box where it has a fuse or circuit breaker. A white, neutral wire and a black, hot wire lead from connections in the box, usually located inside the conduit, through the walls of your house to the area they serve. There they are connected to four or five wall outlets and perhaps two or three ceiling fixtures and wall switches.

The conduit arrives at the point where the first wall outlet is mounted. Here it is attached to a small rectangular metal box, in which the wall outlet itself is protected. The wires are connected to the outlet, and then continue, through more conduit, to the next box. The conduit and the boxes thus provide a kind of protective tunnel inside of which the current-carrying wires run.

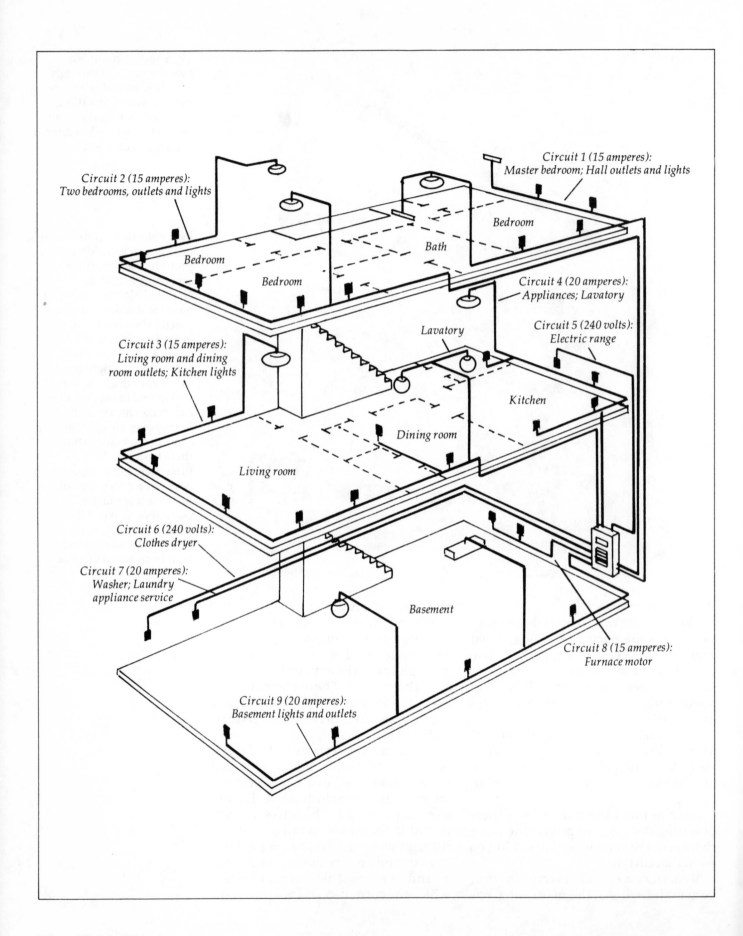

Circuit 2 (15 amperes):
Two bedrooms, outlets and lights

Circuit 1 (15 amperes):
Master bedroom; Hall outlets and lights

Bedroom

Bedroom

Bath

Bedroom

Bedroom

Circuit 4 (20 amperes):
Appliances; Lavatory

Circuit 3 (15 amperes):
Living room and dining
room outlets; Kitchen lights

Lavatory

Circuit 5 (240 volts):
Electric range

Kitchen

Dining room

Living room

Circuit 6 (240 volts):
Clothes dryer

Circuit 7 (20 amperes):
Washer; Laundry
appliance service

Basement

Circuit 8 (15 amperes):
Furnace motor

Circuit 9 (20 amperes):
Basement lights and outlets

In some areas, instead of conduit, the wires may be carried inside armored cable, also called BX cable, or inside heavily insulated nonmetallic cable.

Electric wire

Electric wire is like water pipe — the larger the wire's diameter, the more current it can carry. And also like water pipe, it has a maximum load. We give wire a number according to its diameter. These numbers run from 0 to 18: 0, 2, 3, 4, 6, 8, 10, etc. Zero represents the largest wire, and 18, the smallest wire. (Although wire comes in odd-numbered sizes, the even-numbered sizes are the more frequently used.)

Some wire is stranded, that is, it is made up of a number of small wires twisted together. When you see a single number, 18 for example, this refers to a solid wire. If you see the number 18/30, this refers to a stranded wire and means that 30 strands of No. 18 wire make up the wire. The reason stranded wire is made is that very thick wire, numbers 8, 6, 4, 2, and 0, is not very flexible and becomes hard to handle. Strands of smaller wire provide the correct electrical capacity and still remain flexible.

You can buy either copper or aluminum wire, but copper has some advantages. Copper has less resistance than aluminum, so you can use a smaller copper wire to get the same current-carrying capacity. For example, you use a No. 14 copper wire to carry 15 amps. You must use a No. 12 aluminum wire to get the same capacity. (See the accompanying chart, "Current Capacity of Wire.") Copper also tends to be a little less brittle — it bends more before breaking.

For wiring or rewiring household circuits (general-purpose and appliance circuits), use solid wire, Nos. 14, 12, and 10 in copper, or Nos. 12, 10, and 8 in aluminum. Use stranded wire in making extension cords and power cords for lamps and appliances.

Current Capacity of Wire*		
Wire Size	Amperes Copper	Aluminum
No. 14	15	-
No. 12	20	15
No. 10	30	25
No. 8	40	30
No. 6	55	40
No. 4	70	55
No. 3	80	65
No. 2	95	75
No. 1	110	85
No. 0	125	100

*The wire size is the *minimum* gauge that should be used for the amperage listed. You can use the next larger size gauge.

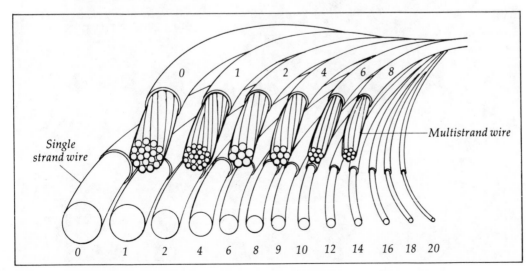

The larger the diameter of an electrical wire, the more current it can carry. Most house wiring is done with Nos. 10, 12, or 14 solid wire. The No. 14 is the minimum wire for a 15-amp circuit. (The larger the number, the smaller the wire.) Multistrand wires are more flexible than solid wires and are commonly used in appliance power cords and extension cords. When buying multistrand wire, check its ampere rating by looking at the label on the wire spool.

Voltage drop

Remember that wire resists the flow of current through it. The loss of voltage because of the resistance in a long run of wire due to resistance is called voltage drop.

The formula for computing voltage drop is the rated resistance of the wire multiplied by the amps it is to carry. If the wire has a resistance of 1 ohm and is to carry 10 amps, then the voltage drop is 10, computed by multiplying 1 x 10. If you have 115-volt service, subtract the voltage drop $(115 - 10 = 105$ volts) to find out what voltage reaches the appliance at the end of this wire. This is fairly low voltage and the voltage drop may affect the way the appliance works. However, you don't have to memorize this formula or use it for selecting wire for your job. The wire specified in the "Current Capacity" chart applies to runs up to 50 feet. For each additional 50-foot run, select a wire one gauge thicker. Thus, if the run is to be 80 feet, use a No. 10 wire instead of a No. 12. This will compensate for the voltage drop.

A situation in which voltage drop can be critical is in the use of very long extension cords, especially in the yard when you are using a mower, drill, saw, or chain saw. You might use a 100-foot extension, plugging it into an outlet that is already 50 feet from the main service box. If the wire in the extension cord is too small, you may not get enough power to operate the unit or to get the best service from it. When buying a long extension cord, get one that can carry the planned load. Check the ampere rating of the appliance you expect to use, then refer to the accompanying "Extension Cord" chart.

Extension Cords			
Length of cord	Light load to 7 amps	Medium Load 7 to 10 amps	Heavy Load 10 to 15 amps
To 25 feet	No. 18 wire	No. 16 wire	No. 14 wire
To 50 feet	No. 16 wire	No. 14 wire	No. 12 wire
To 100 feet	No. 14 wire	No. 12 wire	No. 10 wire

When using long extension cords of 50 feet or more, remember that there is a considerable drop in voltage in long runs of wire due to resistance. If the wire in the extension cord is too small, the voltage drop may be great enough to inhibit the effectiveness of your appliance. Get a heavy-duty extension cord for use with outdoor appliances.

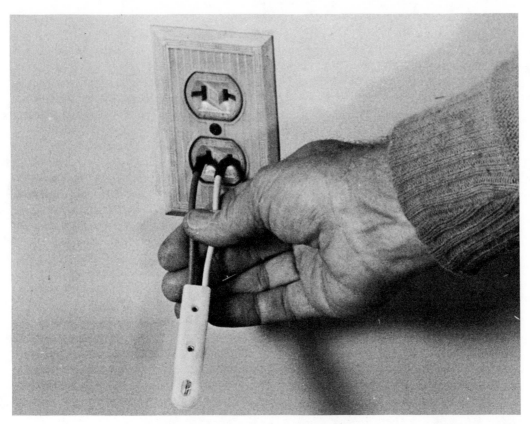

Above and below:
A test light can be useful in unraveling electrical mysteries. It comes in many configurations but consists usually of two probes and a small light. Insert both probes into the prong holes in a wall outlet. If the light glows, there is power in the circuit. The tester can be used to make a number of current and ground tests; read the instructions, which come with it.

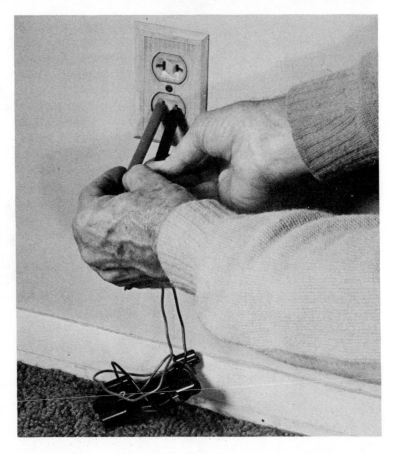

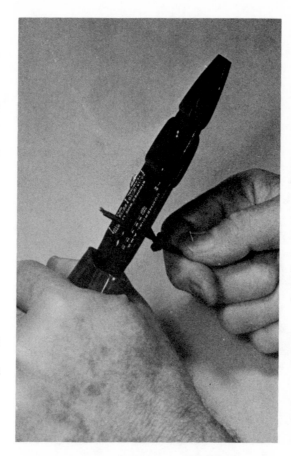

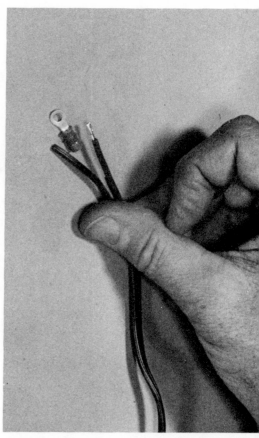

Right:
The wire stripper is a tool of many uses. Its primary function is to strip the insulation from the ends of electrical wire. Notches of different sizes, to fit standard wire sizes, are cut into the inside edges of the handle. Put the wire into the proper-size slot, close the handle, and pull the wire; the insulation is stripped off cleanly and quickly.

Far right:
When repairing appliances, you often need to attach a terminal lug to the end of a wire. If you are working with a two-wire cord, such as this one, begin by splitting the two wires, since each wire will have its own lug. Now strip one of the wires to the correct depth. When inserted in the terminal, no bare copper should show below the insulated collar of the lug.

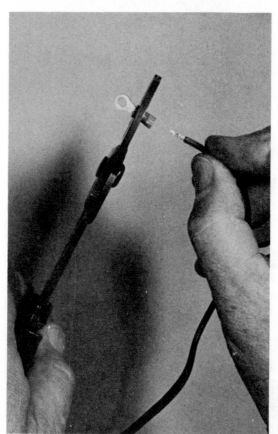

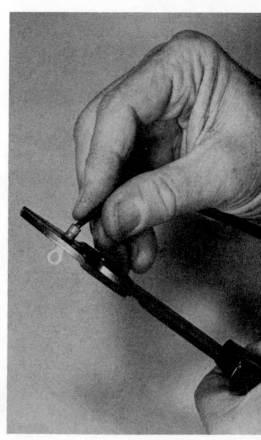

Right:
Gently hold the lug in the crimping slots in the head of the wire stripper, and insert the stripped wire into the lug. Various sizes and styles of lugs are available at electrical supply stores.

Far right:
Squeeze the handle of the wire stripper. This will crimp the body of the lug tightly around the exposed tip of the wire.

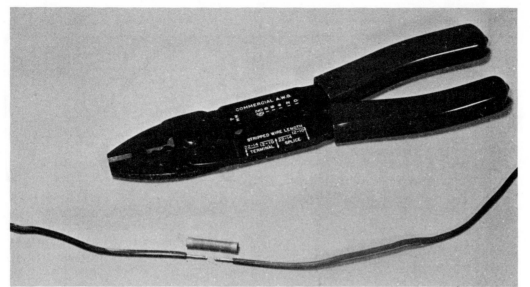

Left and center:
Wire can be joined end to end by using a butt splice. The ends of the wires to be joined are stripped to the correct depth, then each wire is crimped in one end of the lug. A metal sleeve inside the lug insures good electrical contact.

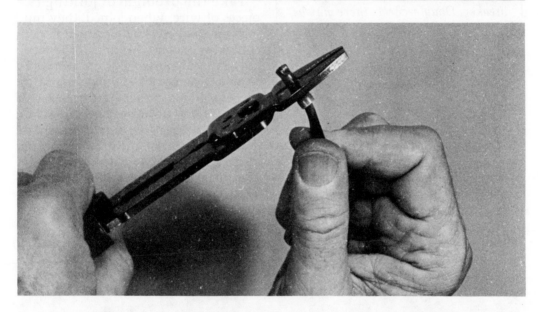

Another way to join wires is to insert the stripped ends into one end of a closed-end splice, and crimp.

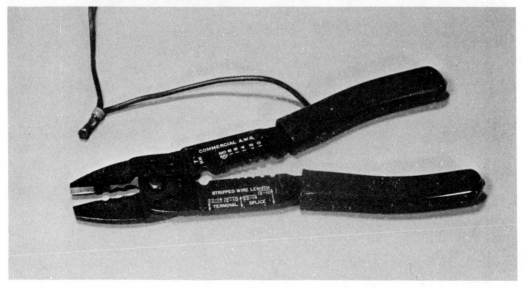

Electrical Methods

There is a neat, clean, and correct way to do almost any task in electrical work, from joining two wires together to connecting runs of conduit. Most of these tasks, taken individually, are easy once you know the right way to do them.

Take the problem of joining two pieces of wire: when joined, they must make a good electrical contact; a poor contact will cause trouble. If the wires are to carry any weight, the joint must be able to support it without separating; the joint shouldn't separate or be jarred loose when the wire is moved, and there should be no wire ends that might penetrate the insulation, which is put over the joint. If you follow the prescribed method of joining two pieces of wire, all of these problems are automatically taken into account.

Joining wires

Joining two wires is called splicing, and the splice must be well made and solid, or later it can cause problems. A loose splice can come apart when the wire is flexed or pulled; and when the wire in a splice makes only loose contact, electricity passing through the splice generates heat. Begin the splice by stripping the ends of the wire. Allow at least an inch and a half of bare wire to give yourself room to work. (Check your local code, because some codes do not permit splices in wires.)

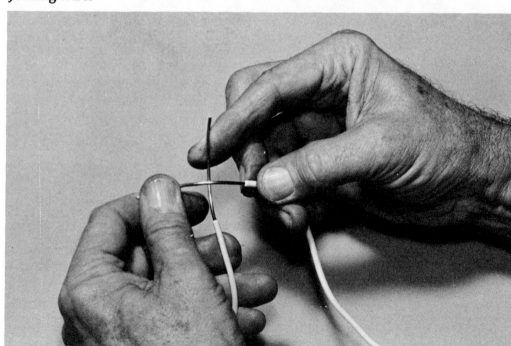

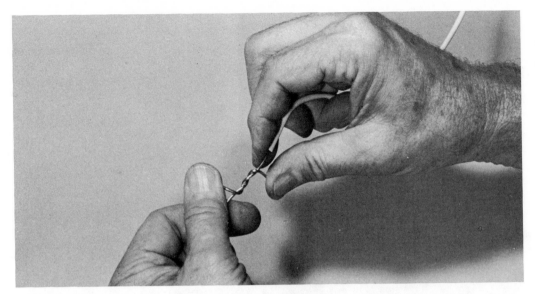

Twist the wires around each other a few turns. The heavier the gauge of the wire, the more difficult it is to make a good splice. The wire in this picture is a No. 14.

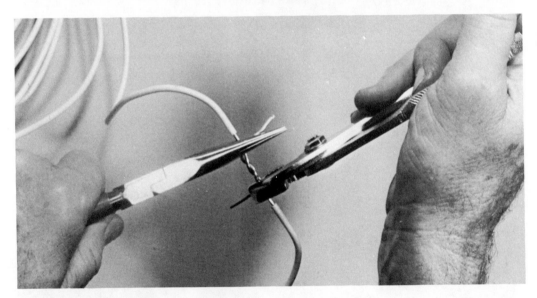

Use two pliers, one to hold the splice and the other to bend the end of the wire around the splice.

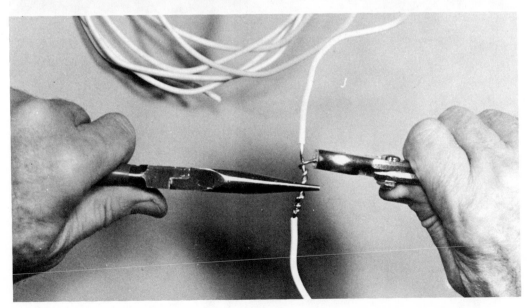

Bend the remainder of the wire into place, and test the splice. It should be firm, with no movement between the joined wires. If you pull on the wires, the splice should hold and show no tendency to pull apart.

Taping wire joints

The object of taping a spliced wire joint is to insulate the splice. Begin by applying the tape to one end of the splice, covering a half inch or so of the wire insulation. Apply the tape at a slight angle so that as you wrap the tape will overlap itself.

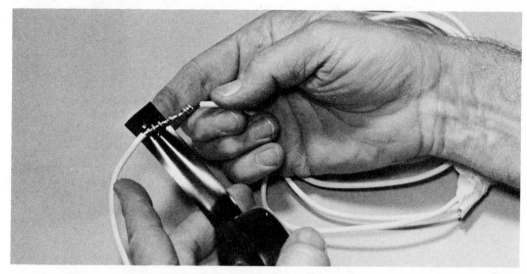

Wrap the tape around the splice permitting it to overlap itself as you proceed. Finish the wrap by covering the wire insulation beyond the splice. Be certain that no sharp ends of wire have punctured the tape and are left exposed. Use a wire cutter to remove any sharp end before you begin wrapping.

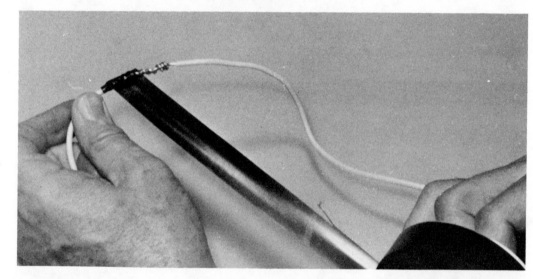

Check the completed wrapping to see that there are no exposed wires anywhere. If necessary, wrap a second time. Splices of this type often are soldered before being taped to insure good electrical contact.

Using solderless connectors

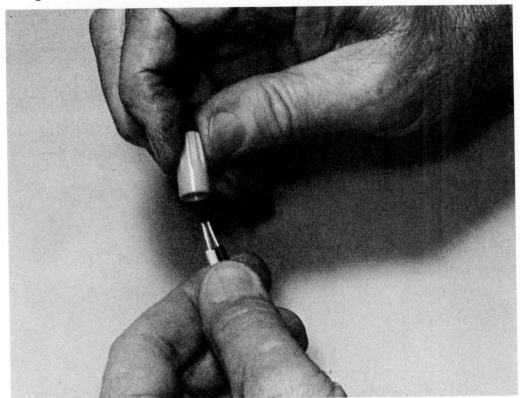

A solderless connector is a plastic cap with a metal spring inside. When the bare ends of two or more wires are inserted into it and twisted, the spring firmly grips the wire and makes a good electrical contact. To use the connector, begin by stripping the wire ends; don't expose too much wire, or the plastic won't cover it.

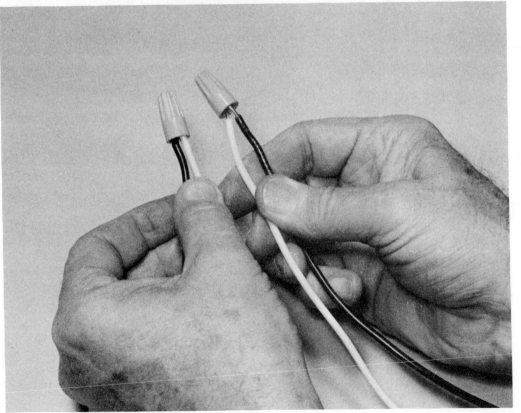

For additional strength twist the wire ends together before inserting them into the connector. (Even if you don't twist them, however, they will make a good electrical connection, but should not be subjected to pulling pressure.) Insert the wire into the cap, and twist the cap until it won't turn any more. In this picture you see a correct and incorrect application. The wire in the connection on the right was stripped too much, and bare copper is exposed below the connector cap. This connection should be remade.

Connecting wire to a fixture

The correct way to begin to connect a wire to a fixture terminal screw is to bend a hook in the wire using needlenose pliers. Make the hook by grasping the wire with the pliers and turning the pliers to bend the wire around the needlenose.

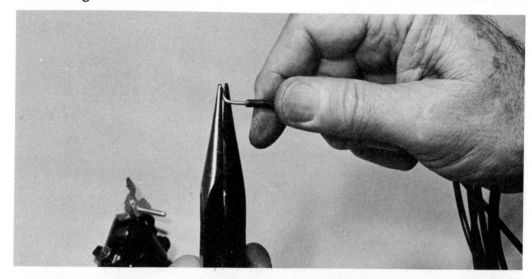

This top view of the hook-making process shows how the wire bends around the nose of the pliers.

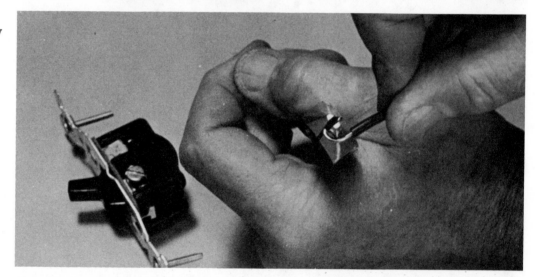

Attach the newly formed hook to a terminal screw by hooking it around the screw with the open mouth of the hook to the right. As you turn toward the open mouth, you tighten the screw. If the hook is put on the opposite way, the wire may slip out from underneath the screwhead as you tighten it.

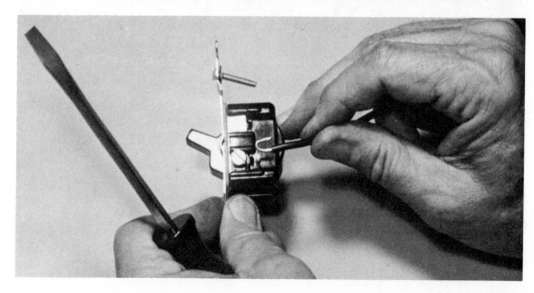

Making an Underwriters' Laboratories electrical knot

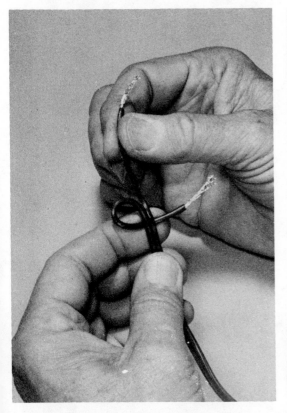

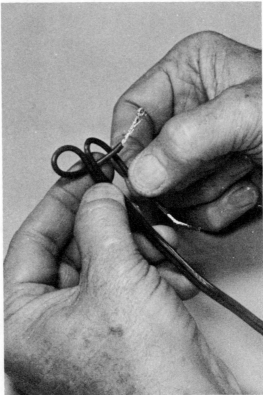

Far left:
Always use an Underwriters' Laboratories electrical knot to prevent putting pressure on the electrical contacts when a power cord is pulled. To make the knot, pull a foot or so of wire through the plug; split about 3 inches of wire, as shown. Begin the knot by looping the wire in the left hand behind the wire in the right hand.

Left:
Bend the right-hand wire down behind the left-hand one.

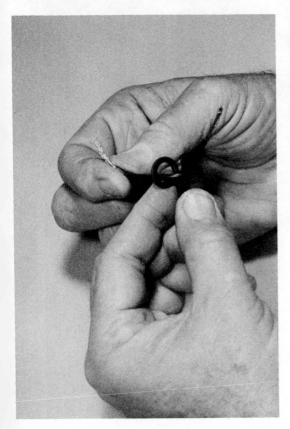

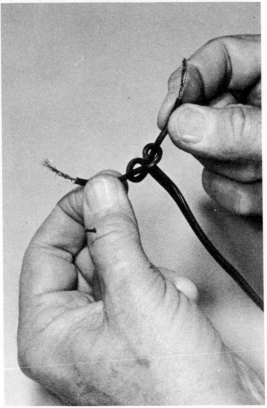

Far left:
Bring the right-hand wire around under the left-hand wire, and pass it through the original loop you made.

Left:
Pull both wires to draw the knot tight. Be sure there is enough wire beyond the knot so you can make your connections inside the plug. It is better to have too much wire than too little, since you can always cut off the excess.

Right:
Before pulling the knot down into the plug, twist the stranded wire into a solid wire to eliminate frazzled ends.

Far right:
Pull the power cord, and draw the knot down into the plug. The completed knot should be small enough so that it fits into the plug between the prongs. You may find it necessary to pull the knot tighter to achieve this.

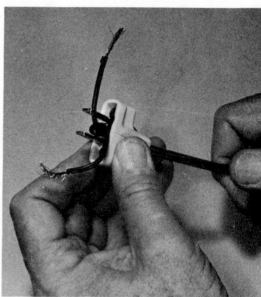

Cutting armored cable

Armored cable, sometimes called BX, is a flexible, metal-shielded set of wires (a white and a black wire plus a ground wire) used for extending circuits and for doing other homewiring. Many codes insist that new wiring be done with conduit but permit the use of armored cable for additions of new switches or wall outlets. To cut armored cable, use a hacksaw with a fine-toothed blade. Cut through the metal jacket, across one of the ribs; when you have cut through the metal, stop sawing. Take the cable in both hands, and snap it. This will break all but a small section of metal that you cut with the saw. (This is done to avoid accidentally cutting through the insulation of the wire inside the shield.) Finally, pull on the short end of the metal shield. Usually any section 12 inches long or less will pull right off, leaving the wires unshielded and ready for work.

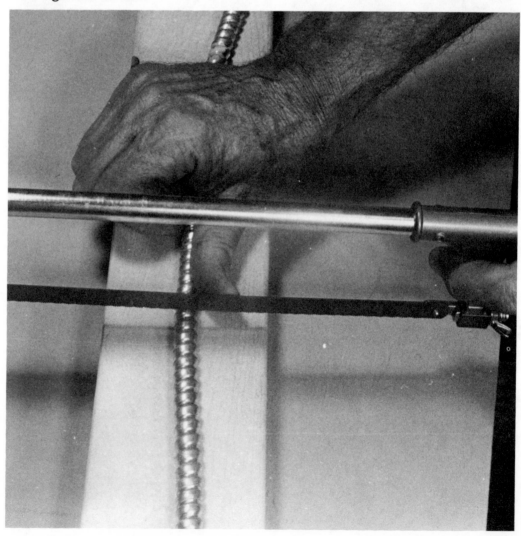

Connecting armored cable

These two paper-wrapped wires are the electrical wires of the cable; the silver unshielded wire is the ground wire. At right, is a small bushing (a lining used to reduce friction). Whenever the raw end of armored cable is attached to anything, a bushing should be inserted to protect the wires from the metal edges.

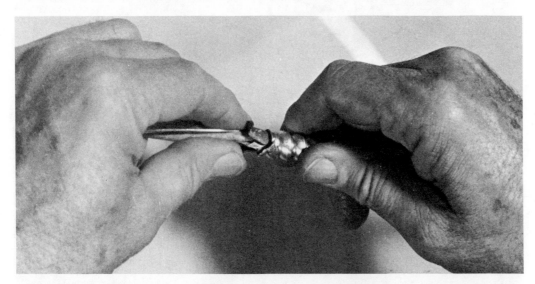

Right and below:
The bushing is pushed down between the wire and the metal covering. If you do your own wiring and then have it inspected, these bushings are among the things the inspector will look for.

Right:
Armored cable is attached to a junction box by means of a connector, shown here. To attach a connector, bend the ground wire back, and slip the connector over the wires, the bushing, and first half inch of the metal shield of the cable. The connector is then fastened to the cable by tightening the screw.

Far right:
Wrap the ground wire around the screw, and tighten the screw to make a solid contact. Do not neglect to make this ground connection or you will destroy the continuous ground of your circuit. After tightening the screw, clip off any excess ground wire.

To make an opening in a junction box, select the point where you want the armored cable to enter the box. Then, using a screwdriver and either the butt of your hand or a hammer, knock loose the tab in the hole.

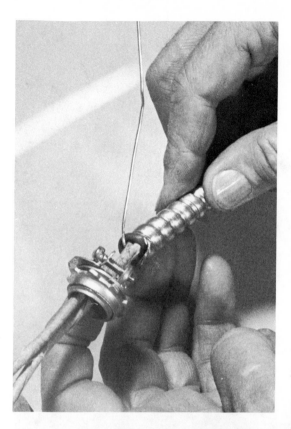

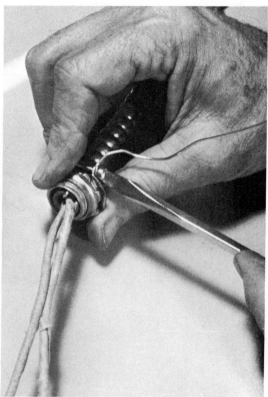

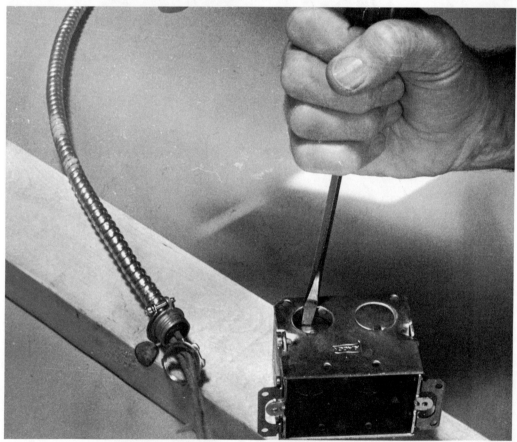

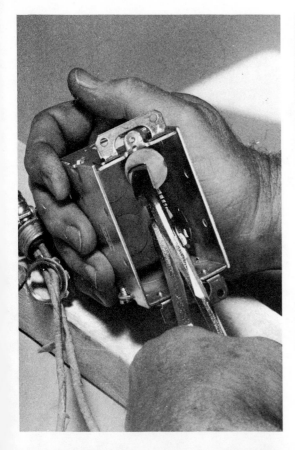

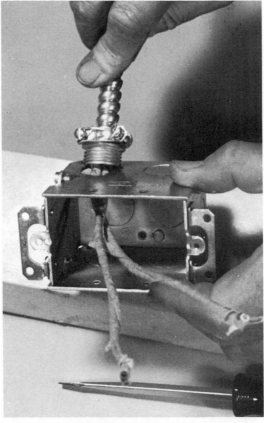

Far left:
Grasp the tab with pliers, and twist it a few times; it will come off.

Left:
Insert the connector into the opening in the box. Normally, the junction box is mounted in the wall. Here, it is detached for photographic purposes.

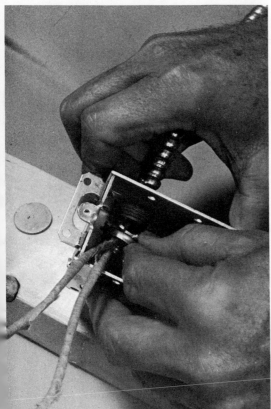

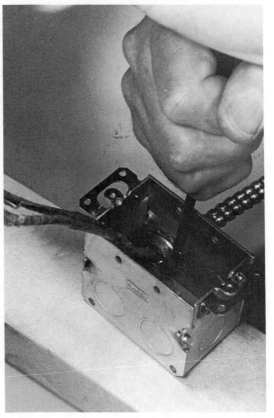

Far left:
Once the threaded end of the connector is in the box, slip the connector ring nut over the wires, down to the threads. Turn it with your fingertips.

Left:
Finally, insert a screwdriver into one of the notches in the edge of the ring nut, and tap it to tighten.

Connecting nonmetallic cable

Right:
Nonmetallic cable is a heavy plastic-protected cable inside of which are electric wires. Cable can be bought with different combinations of wire, but for normal circuit wiring buy cable with three wires—a hot wire, a neutral wire, and a ground wire. The first task in connecting nonmetallic cable is to strip away the heavy outside insulation. A single-edge razor blade is handy for this job. As you cut, be careful not to cut into the insulation around the individual wires inside the cable.

Far right:
Slip a connector into place, once the three wires are stripped of their outside protective jacket. This connector is similar to that used to connect armored cable to a junction box; be sure you buy the right type of connector.

Right:
Insert the connector into the box, and thread on a ring nut with your finger; tighten it with a screwdriver.

Far right:
In another view of the completed connection, note that the red, or ground, wire must be attached to the box, while the other two wires are used to make the electrical connection. The ground wire can be connected to the box by means of a small clip or by means of a screw driven into a hole in the back or side of the box. Some boxes come equipped with this screw already in place. *Do not neglect to make this ground connection.*

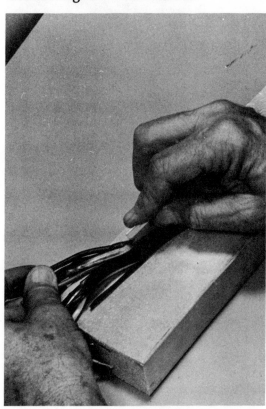

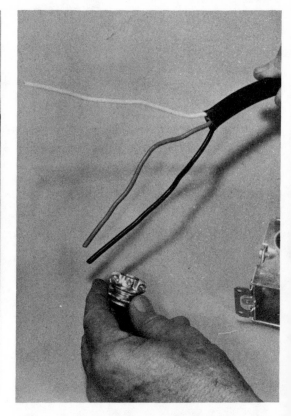

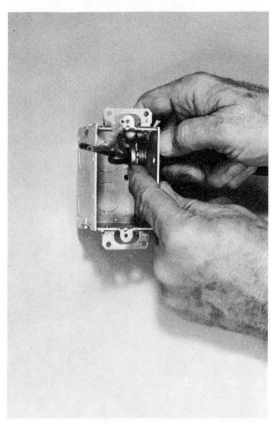

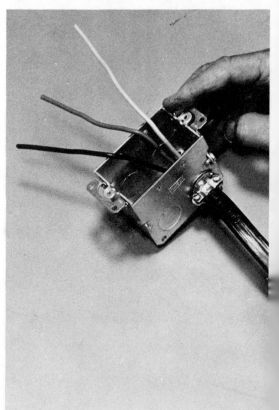

Working with conduit

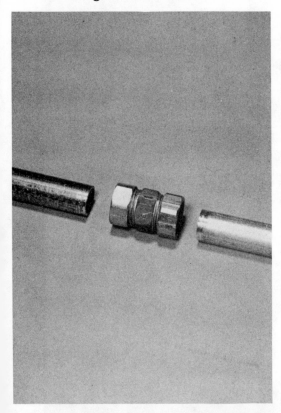

Far left:
A thin-wall conduit is a thin tube used for carrying electrical wires throughout a home. It is easily cut and easily bent, yet strong enough to give good wire protection. Conduit is not threaded like ordinary pipelike tube but is joined by slip fittings; insert the conduit into the fitting, and tighten the nut.

Left:
The fitting that joins conduit to a junction box has one end threaded to fit into the junction box where it is held in place by a ring nut. These two views show the connector properly assembled (at top) and the nut and expansion ring, by which the conduit is gripped, pulled apart.

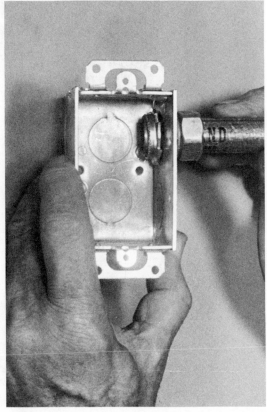

Far left:
To join conduit to a junction box, insert the conduit in the connector; tighten the connector on the conduit.

Left:
Once the connector is inserted in the box, the ring nut is threaded on and tightened by inserting a screwdriver in one of the notches in the edge of the ring nut and tapping.

Thin-wall conduit is easily cut with this special cutter, which is clamped around the conduit. You can rent a cutter instead of buying one if you don't do much electrical work.

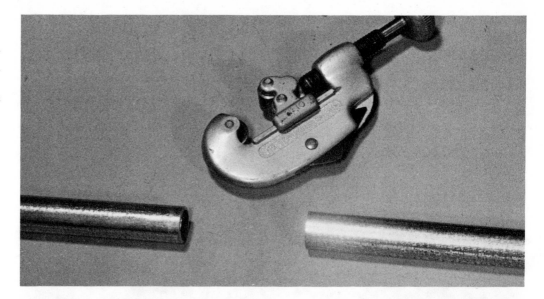

To cut the conduit, tighten the cutter by turning the knurled nut in the handle. As you tighten, force the cutter to revolve around the conduit. The sharp cutting blade will cut a groove that deepens with each revolution, making a smooth and quick cut. After the conduit has been cut, use pliers to remove any burrs that might remain around the edge of the cut.

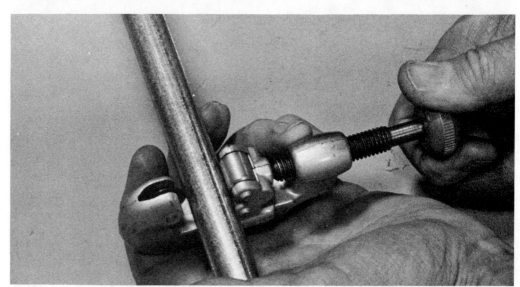

A conduit bender bends conduit readily when you apply pressure to the long handle. The bender is made so that the minimum-radius bend allowed for electrical installation is made automatically.

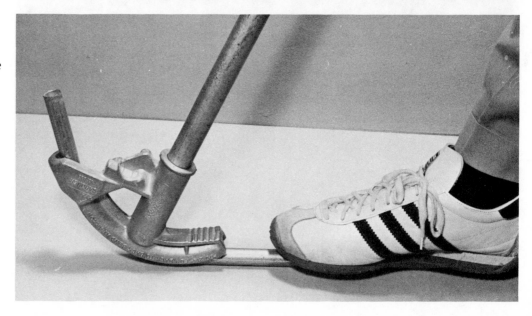

Using a fish tape

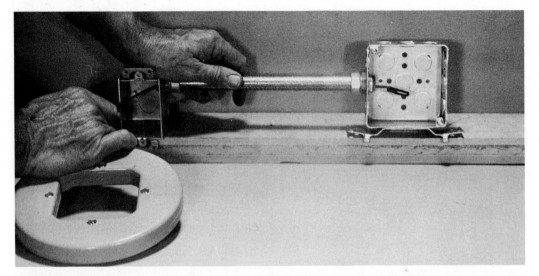

A fish tape is a thin, flexible metal tape with a bent hook on one end, which is usually packaged on some type of convenient reel. Its purpose is to pull wires through conduit or through walls. These two junction boxes were set up to show in principle how a fish tape is used. In this picture, the tape is inserted into the conduit from the left side, and run through the conduit to the box on the right. You can see the hooked end of the fish tape in the box at the right.

The two wires to be drawn through the conduit are hooked around the fish-tape hook. If the run of conduit is not too long and doesn't have too many bends, a good tight bend of the wire around the hook will be enough. If the run is long and full of bends, so that you must pull hard, you should wrap some electrical tape around the wires to hold them on the hook.

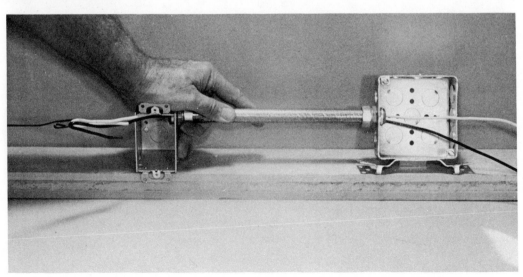

As you pull the fish tape through the conduit, you draw the wires through.

This method demonstrates
how wire should be run
between floors.

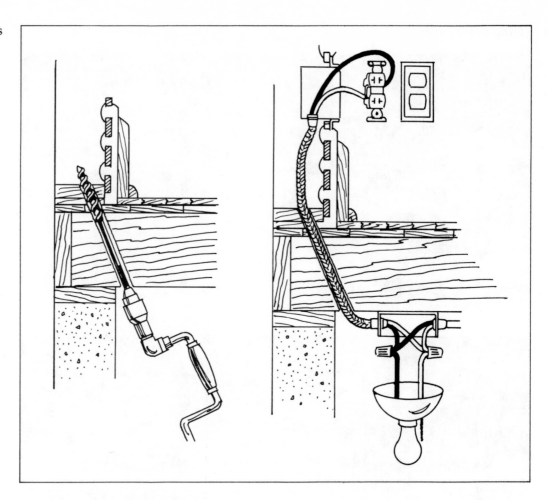

Working on Household Circuits

When doing maintenance or repair on your home's electrical system, keep in mind two basic rules. The first is never work on a circuit without shutting off the power, even if you think the job is so simple that this isn't necessary. Turn off the power anyway. The second rule is to perform each task correctly, step by step. Each correct method has been developed for reasons of safety and for the good performance of the system. Taking shortcuts can prove dangerous.

Proceed slowly with your work. Read all directions first, and then plan your work. Always purchase parts and supplies before you begin, and if you have planned carefully, you should know exactly what you need.

Replacing a switch

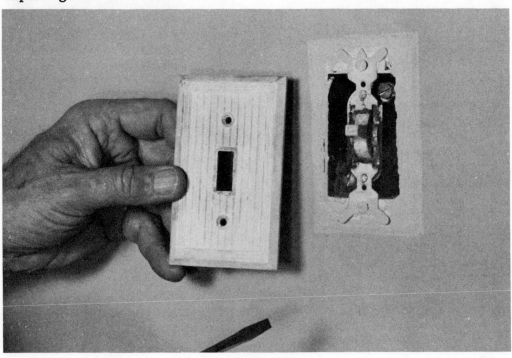

When a switch gets sticky or must be flipped several times before the lights go on, it should be replaced. TURN OFF THE ELECTRIC CURRENT; NEVER WORK ON ANYTHING ALIVE WITH ELECTRICITY. The following procedure applies to replacing a regular switch either with a mercury (silent type) switch or with a dimmer switch. In each case, check the instructions on the switch package to be certain the wiring is the same before you begin. Then, remove the wall plate by removing the two screws that hold it in place.

Right:
Remove the two screws that hold the switch to the box.

Far right:
Pull the switch from the box. If heavy-gauge wire has been used in the wiring, pull hard enough to bend the wires and bring the switch all the way out so that you can work on it. Remove the old switch by removing the two electrical contact wires. If you take the screw all the way out, the wires stay bent, which makes connecting the new switch easier.

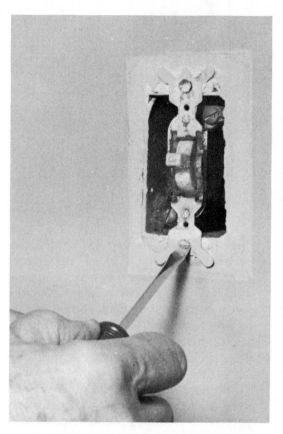

Right:
Put in the new switch by attaching the two electrical wires. The white wire should be attached to the light-colored screw.

Far right:
Press the switch into the box. You may have to bend the wires a bit first. Work with it until the switch sits neatly in the box. You will note that the screws holding the switch to the box go through slots, rather than holes, in the arms of the switch. This is done so that you can adjust the position of the switch slightly before finally tightening the screws.

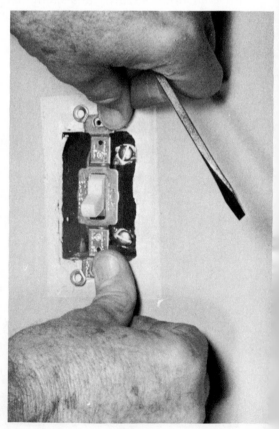

Replacing a wall outlet

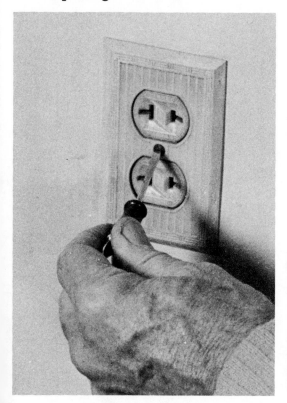

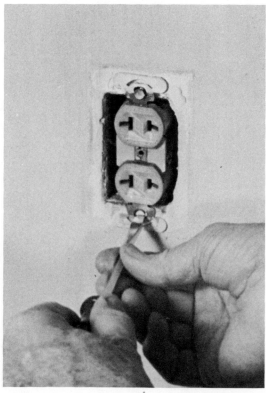

Far left:
Replacing a standard wall outlet is similar to replacing a switch. Begin by removing the wall plate.

Left:
Remove the old receptacle by removing the two screws holding it to the box.

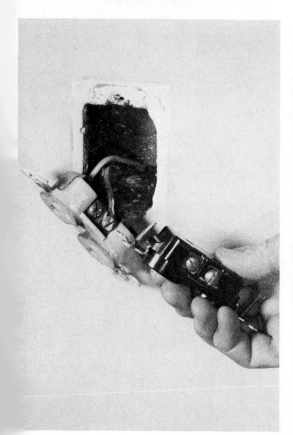

Far left:
Pull the old receptacle from the box. Here, the new receptacle is shown alongside the old one.

Left:
The old receptacle is removed by taking out the screws to which the electrical wires are connected. The new receptacle is then put into place, the electrical wires are slipped around the terminal screws, and the screws are tightened. The white wire is connected to the light-colored screw.

Right:
The new receptacle is pushed into the box and tightened.

Far right:
The wall plate is screwed into place, and the installation is complete.

Converting a wall outlet to a grounded receptacle

Right:
The kitchen wall outlet is one into which a good many appliances are plugged. A three-prong converter plug can be used whenever an appliance with a three-prong power plug is used, but to get rid of this nuisance, the outlet can be converted to a grounded receptacle. First, **turn off the power** either by flipping the circuit breaker in the main service box to "Off" or by unscrewing the fuse for this circuit. Then, unscrew the wall plate.

Far right:
Pull the old receptacle from the box, and remove the screws holding the electrical wires.

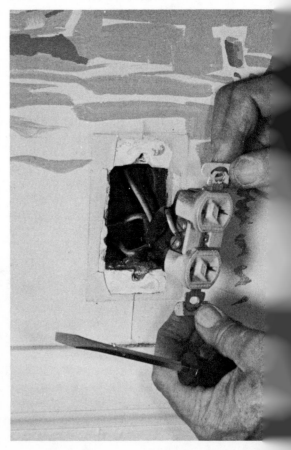

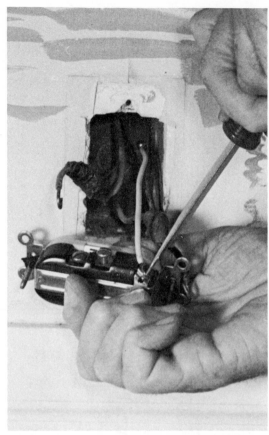

Far left:
To attach the new ground wire, cut a length of wire the same size as used in your circuit (No. 10, 12, or 14), and strip the insulation from both ends. The wire should be about 6 inches long. Make a loop at one end, and attach this to the box by means of the screw you see in the back of the box. If there is no screw in your box, buy a ground clip; attach the ground wire to it, and clip it to the edge of the box.

Left:
Purchase a grounded receptacle for this installation. The visible difference between a grounded and ungrounded receptacle is that the grounded receptacle has a green-colored scew. This is the screw to which you attach the grounding wire you have already connected to the box.

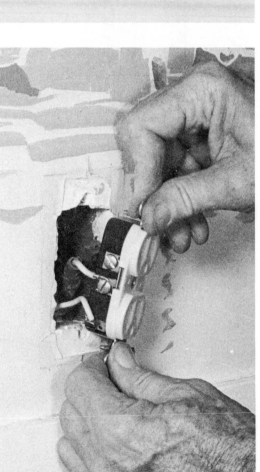

Far left:
Attach the two electrical wires, white and black, making sure the white wire is attached to the light-colored screw on the side of the receptacle.

Left:
Put the receptacle back into the wall box, bending the wires as necessary to make it fit, and replace the wall plate. If there is a continuous ground in the circuit to which you have just wired the receptacle, you do not have to use converter plugs. Use a tester to check to be sure that the circuit is grounded.

Adding new wall outlets

You can use as many wall outlets as you need on any circuit as a matter of convenience. However, whatever number outlets you have, you shouldn't overload the circuit by using more appliances at one time than it can take. There are several ways to increase the number of outlets with a minimum amount of work. One is to go straight through an existing wall outlet in one room, and install a wall outlet in the room on the other side of the wall. The procedure is simple. Measure carefully to locate the new wall outlet exactly opposite the old one. Then cut an opening in the wall for a junction box, and cut a short length of conduit to connect the two boxes as shown. Finally, make the electrical connections, white wire to light-colored screw and black wire to darker brass-colored screw.

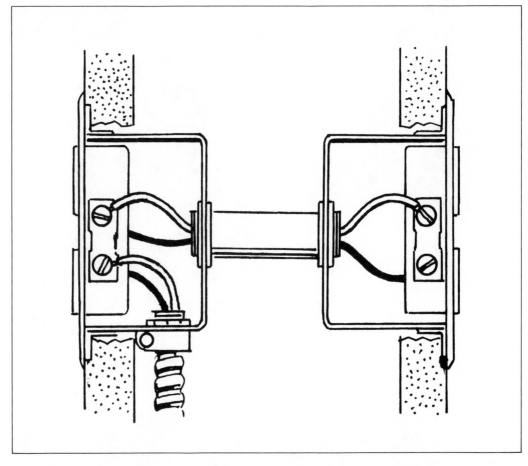

Installing a new lateral-run outlet

To install a new outlet five or six feet from an existing one, run a wire from the existing outlet to the new outlet. Chisel a groove between the outlets, cutting through the plaster or plasterboard and notching the 2x4s behind the plaster. The wire, which is usually armored cable, is fitted into this notch. After the new wall outlet is completely wired, fill the notch with plaster. It's a bit messy, but the convenience of the new outlet is worth it.

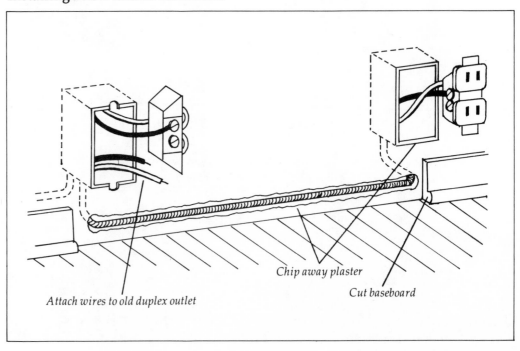

Chip away plaster

Cut baseboard

Attach wires to old duplex outlet

Installing a new outlet from a switch

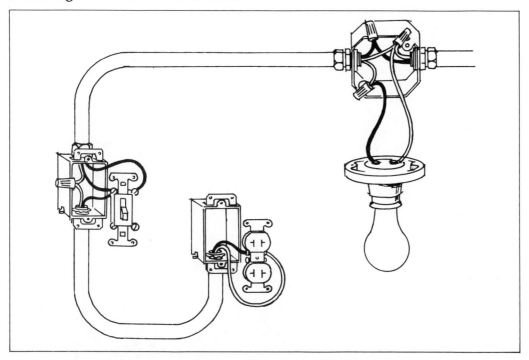

Add a new wall outlet by working from an existing switch and ceiling fixture. In most cases, ceiling fixtures are controlled by simple "drop" switches, that is, the switch is dropped from the ceiling fixture, and two wires run through the conduit from the fixture to the switch. You need to add a third wire in this conduit run. Study this wiring diagram for a few moments to see how the third wire is used.

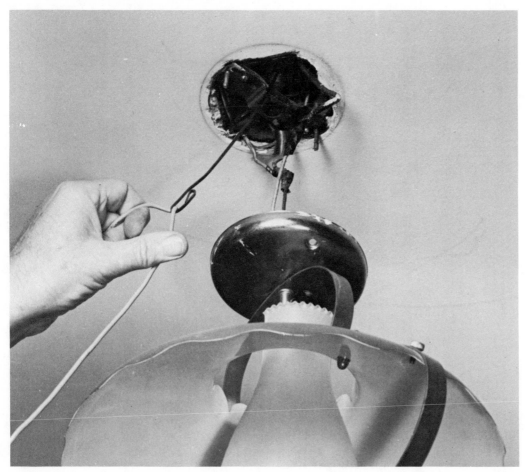

Remove the wall plate, take the switch out of the box, and remove the screws holding the ceiling fixture. Let it down gently, since the weight of the fixture will be entirely on the wires. If the fixture is heavy, have someone support it, or disconnect it completely, and reconnect it after the wiring of the switch has been completed. Insert the hook end of the fish tape into the conduit at the switch box leading to the ceiling fixture; slowly push it through the conduit. You will meet a little resistance as the tape turns the corner at the ceiling, but push a bit, and the tape will make the turn. The tape will come out through the box of the ceiling fixture, shown here. Attach a wire to the tape; make sure the wire is long enough to go all the way to the switch and also have an extra foot at each end.

Right:
Keep pulling on the fish tape, using a steady pressure to draw the wire through the conduit. You now have a new wire in the conduit from the ceiling fixture to the wall switch.

Far right:
Before connecting the wires in the ceiling fixture study the existing wires carefully and refer to the wiring diagram, "Installing a new outlet from a switch." Identify each wire, and understand how it should be connected. In this photo, the three wires to be connected by means of a solderless connector have been pulled out and stripped.

Right:
The connection is made using solderless connectors. Note that the three wires and the wire from the fixture itself are joined in the large solderless connector. You can now push all the wiring back up into the ceiling box, and put the fixture back in place.

Far right:
Next, at the point on the wall where you want the new outlet, measure carefully, and mark its location.

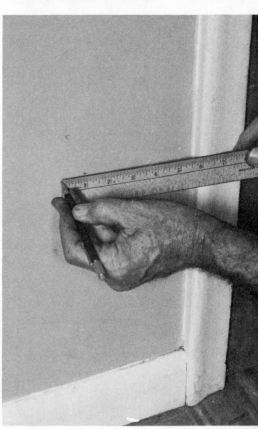

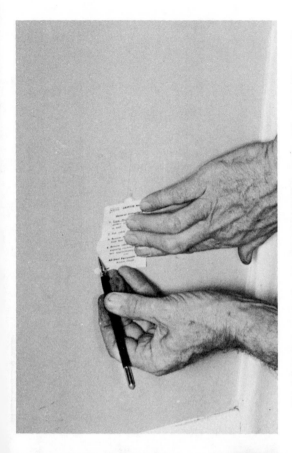

Far left:
A cardboard template should come with each wall box you buy. Position this template on the wall, and draw an outline around it.

Left:
Using an electric drill, drill on the inside of the lines you have drawn. Make most of the cutout with the drill, or simply make an entry hole at each corner, and complete the cutout with a keyhole or power saber saw.

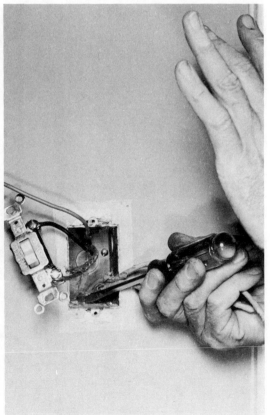

Far left:
The finished hole, cut exactly as indicated by the template, makes allowances for "ears" on the wall box. The box, shown here, has two side pieces with screws in them. Put the box into the new opening, and tighten the screws with a screwdriver. The two metal pieces on the side contact as you turn the screws and grip the wall to hold the box solidly in place.

Left:
To run wire from the box down to the new outlet, tap out the tab in the bottom of the box with a screwdriver and your hand.

Left and right:
Drop a piece of string down through the opening in the bottom of the wall switch box until you can see it through the new opening you have just cut for the wall outlet. Pull the string out through the wall outlet opening.

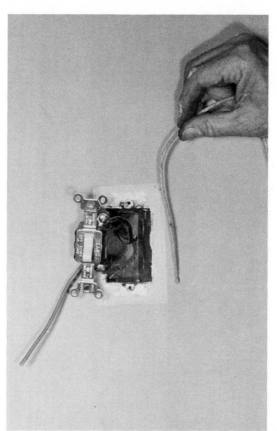

Cut a length of armored cable to run from the wall switch box to the new wall outlet box. Install a box connector, including the ground wire connection and the bushing, before running it into the wall.

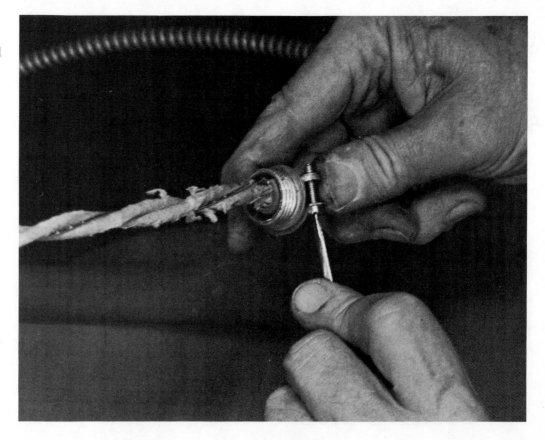

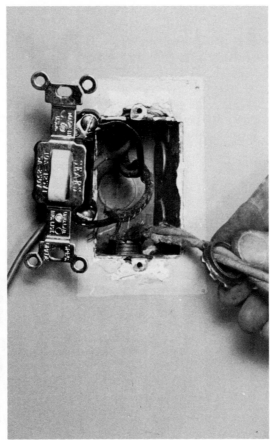

Far left:
Tie the string to this armored cable, and pull the cable up through the wall.

Left:
You may have to jiggle the string a bit, but you can now pull the armored cable connector into the wall switch box, as shown. Slip a ring nut over the wires into the box. Tighten this nut over the connector.

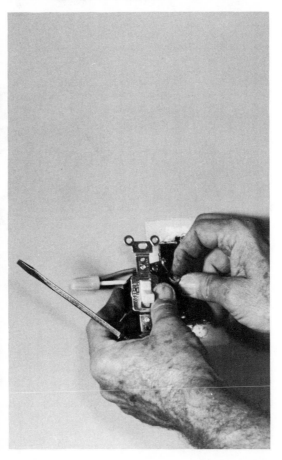

Far left:
Complete the installation of the wall outlet by attaching the wires, inserting the receptacle in the box, and putting the wall plate in place.

Left:
Reinstall the switch in the wall box. Carefully study the diagram of the three-way switch, which follows, to make the proper electrical connections.

Installing a three-way switch

Three-way switches are used to control a single light from two different points. For example, a stairway light, which is controlled by a switch at the bottom of the stairs and by another at the top, can be turned on as you start up the stairs and turned off when you reach the top. The only difference between two-way and three-way switches is the way in which they are wired. Two types of three-way switch wiring are shown. At left, both switches are beyond the light in the household circuit, and a three-wire cable is used between the two switches. At right, the light is between the two switches in the circuit, and a three-wire cable runs from each switch to the light. Follow the diagram that illustrates the type of connection you need to make. (Remember, you must connect the black, white, and red wires as directed.) Locate the light- and dark-colored terminals on your switches. And, although your switches may vary slightly from the ones illustrated, the connections should be made in the same way, that is, by joining the white and red wires to the light-colored terminals, and the black wire to the dark-colored terminal. Finally, in order to identify a three-way cable, the ends of the white wire coming from the switch should be painted black at the switch and at the light.

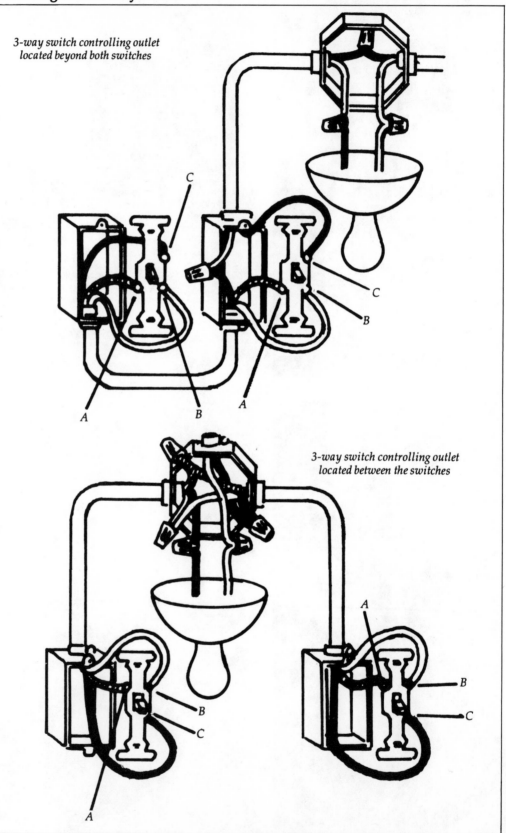

3-way switch controlling outlet located beyond both switches

3-way switch controlling outlet located between the switches

Changing a ceiling fixture

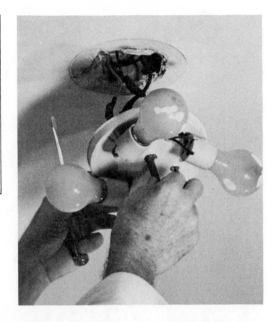

A ceiling fixture is attached to a junction box in the ceiling. Many lightweight fixtures are held in place by two screws threaded into a metal support bar stretched across the opening of the box. To drop the fixture, simply remove the screws. Heavier fixtures are attached to the box by a threaded pipe nipple, as this one is. When the nut is removed, the fixture drops down. In either case, once the fixture has dropped, the wires can be disconnected and the fixture taken down.

You can install a pipe support to replace the metal bar by using a screwdriver to tap out the center tab in the back of the ceiling box and installing a threaded fixture stud in the hole. A U-shape extender known as a "hickey" is threaded tightly over the fixture stud. These two fittings, used together, give you a solid attachment directly to the ceiling box and will bear the weight of a heavy fixture. (Both fittings are for sale at electrical supply stores.)

The hickey, together with a threaded nipple, is attached to the ceiling fixture. You can buy threaded nipples in various lengths. Use a length that supports the fixture at the proper distance below the ceiling so the cover plate fits snugly against the ceiling. You may have to try several nipples before finding the right length. The two wires from the fixture go up through this nipple and emerge in the ceiling box through the open side of the hickey. After stripping the ends of these wires, join them to the same wires in the box to which the old fixture was connected by using solderless connectors, as shown. Tuck all the wires into the box, push the cover plate up against the ceiling, and tighten the nut that holds it in place.

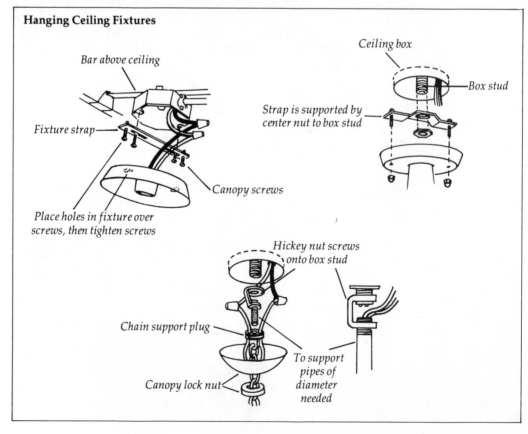

Hanging Ceiling Fixtures

Bar above ceiling

Fixture strap

Place holes in fixture over screws, then tighten screws

Canopy screws

Ceiling box

Box stud

Strap is supported by center nut to box stud

Hickey nut screws onto box stud

Chain support plug

Canopy lock nut

To support pipes of diameter needed

Cover plates on ceiling fixtures vary in size. If the cover plate on the new fixture is smaller than the old one, paint the ceiling to hide the marks left by the old plate.

Installing a swag lamp

Far left:
A swag lamp is the easiest type of ceiling fixture to install because you don't have to run any wires through the ceiling. The lamp's wiring is woven through the chain, where it is nearly invisible, and the lamp can be plugged into a regular wall outlet.

Left:
The hook from which the lamp is suspended is mounted in the ceiling, preferably screwed into a ceiling joist, which provides solid support. You can locate a joist by tapping on the ceiling; the thumps you make sound hollow between the joists and solid when you tap right over a joist. Once you think you have located a joist, double-check yourself by drilling a small hole at that point. If the drill meets wood, you have the right spot.

It is best to find a ceiling joist to support the swag lamp hook because of the weight of the lamp. But the hook that supports the chain near the wall can be supported by a toggle bolt installed through a hole drilled in the plaster, as shown. Take your swag hook to the hardware dealer, and he can supply the proper toggle bolt and the threaded rod needed. Drill a hole in the ceiling large enough for the folded toggle to pass through. Once through the hole, the arms of the toggle spring open and provide the support you need.

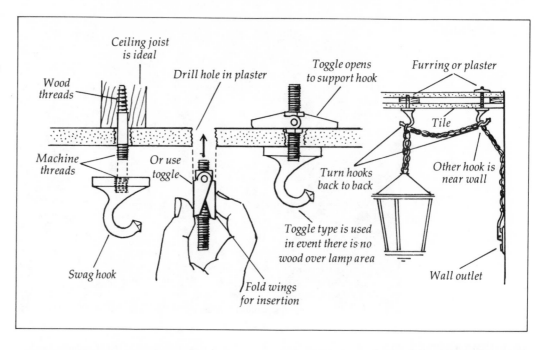

Installing outdoor lighting

Your home should be well lighted on the outside for beauty, safety, and security. Police say that good lighting is one of the best burglar deterrents. All entryways, walks, and passageways should be lighted, as should the perimeter of your home and windows where burglars might attempt to gain access. All exterior lighting should be controlled from switches inside the house.

There are two basic types of exterior lighting — that which is attached to the house, like this porch light, and that which is away from the house, such as a yard light. Those attached to the house can tie into electrical circuits already in the walls and are simpler and less expensive to install.

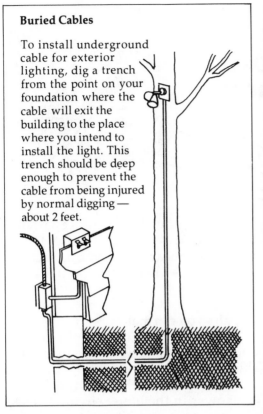

This security spotlight was mounted to provide light for a backyard. Because it is in an exposed position, it is of weatherproof construction. When buying fixtures for outdoor installation, make sure they are of heavy-duty construction, are sealed against water, and have been approved for outdoor use. You should find an Underwriters' Laboratories label on the fixture saying that it can be used in wet or exposed places.

Far left:
In this photo, you can see that a hole was cut in the wall of the house and a junction box installed. The wiring was run from the circuit closest to the installation. A switch was installed inside the home near the door, just behind and below this box. The circular plate, shown, came with the fixture and was attached to the junction box with small screws. The fixture was then held in place by means of long screws that threaded into the openings on the circular plate.

Left:
Enclosed or screened porches should have exterior-type fixtures, since these areas are only partially protected from the elements. This wall outlet is the exterior type, with watertight caps that cover the outlet openings when they aren't in use.

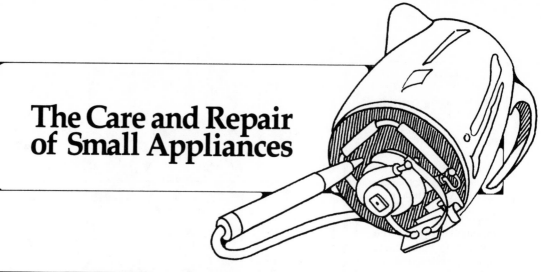

The Care and Repair of Small Appliances

Turn off the electricity at the service entry, either a fuse box or circuit breaker, or unplug the appliance to be repaired. You can't be shocked by electricity when the circuit is defused or the appliance cord has been removed from the outlet.

Most of us have a houseful of small appliances, from electric knives and toothbrushes to toasters and coffee makers. These are fairly simple devices, operating around a small motor, a fan, a heating element, or some combination of these. All have a power cord by which they are connected to a wall outlet, and all have some type of on/off switch or some slightly more sophisticated control that allows you to select one of several settings, such as the light-medium-dark control on a toaster.

In repairing a small appliance, you might think of two electrical sections. The first is from the plug on the power cord through the appliance's power cord to the switch inside the appliance housing. Repairs on this part of the appliance are easy to make and account for a fair percentage of appliance malfunctioning.

The second section is beyond the switch, inside the appliance housing. The current passes through the switch and goes to the motor or heating element, perhaps through some kind of governing device. Several different kinds of motors are used in small appliances, as are several methods of governing speed or heat. Repairing these requires some expertise. If the problem appears to be in this section beyond the switch, have a repairman handle it.

Repairs you can make

When you switch an appliance on and nothing happens, do the following things:

- Start by suspecting that there is no power in the house circuit. Check the fuse or circuit breaker or take the appliance to a wall outlet served by another circuit, and plug it in there. (Don't leave any stone unturned. Flip a couple of light switches to be sure that there is current somewhere in the house, and that you aren't living with a power failure.) You can test the wall outlet by plugging a small table lamp into it and turning on the light.
- If you are satisfied that there is current coming to the wall outlet, turn your attention to the plug and power cord of the appliance. Is the plug in good shape? Are the prongs bent? Are the wires connected inside it? If the plug is of the molded type, so that you can't see the internal connections, it is sometimes worthwhile to begin by replacing it. Is the cord cracked or worn?

Believe it or not, these simple steps can save you some repair money. Every service man has stories about traveling five miles only to replace a fuse or straighten bent prongs on a plug. These stories match the ones told by auto mechanics who have been called because a car won't start, only to find that the car is out of gas. In both cases, you still pay for the service call.

By taking these steps, you assure yourself that there is power in the circuit; that the wall outlet is in good shape and passes the current along to the appliance plug; that the appliance plug is making contact in the wall and is passing the current into the power cord; and that the cord is unbroken and is carrying the current to the appliance switch.

Opening the appliance

DON'T EVER BEGIN TO TAKE AN APPLIANCE APART UNTIL YOU HAVE UNPLUGGED IT.

The next step is to remove the housing of the appliance in order to examine the switch. Sometimes this means just removing a few clearly visible screws. But other times, you must play detective and hunt for the ways in which the case is held together.

Clues. Look for screws that are hidden under nameplates. Look for press-fitted rings that hold the two halves of a housing together and which must be pried off. If the appliance has rubber or plastic feet, look up inside these; screws may be hiding there or disguised somewhere in the handle. If there is a dial on the switch, it must be pulled off before the housing can be disassembled.

When taking an appliance apart, be careful to remember which screws came for each hole. The assembly screws often are not interchangeable, either in threads or in length. Also, watch for lock washers and gaskets, which must be put back where you found them.

Inside the case

No matter what kind of appliance you are working on, the next step, after removing the housing, is to follow the power cord to the point where its wires are connected to the switch. If the power cord inside the housing is frayed, cracked, or worn, replace it,

even if that isn't the source of the present problem. Are the power cord wires in solid contact with the switch, attached with either tight screws or solder? A faulty connection here is one common source of trouble.

Now look at the switch itself. Operate it a few times, and watch closely to see how it works. Does it seem to operate properly? Is it clean, or do the contact points appear burned or discolored? Has dirt, oil, or dust worked its way in and coated the points?

Take the time to clean the points, and be sure a good electrical contact is being made. If the switch is very dirty, the cleaning may solve the problem.

If the contact points are burned or pitted, clean them by using a piece of matchbook cover, running it back and forth between the points. In extreme cases, a couple of passes (light ones) with a very fine emery paper may help.

Sometimes you'll find that the arm of the switch has been bent or has lost its spring. You may be able to correct this by bending it back into position, or you may have to order a new switch from the maker.

If the switch appears good, check all other connections and wiring inside the housing. Are there loose wires? Are all connections tight? Is the wire sound and uncracked, or does the insulation appear broken? You should replace any bad wire, but be sure to replace it with a wire of the same gauge. A hardware store or a radio/TV supply store sells wire.

When you have finished this inspection, reassemble the appliance, being careful to put it back together just the way it came apart. Now turn it on. You may have fixed it. But if you haven't, you can assume that the problem is in the motor or in the governing device, which is a job for a specialist.

Appliance parts

Today most appliance manufacturers are very conscious of the need to supply good after-the-sale service, which includes both repairing appliances and selling parts. You can usually get parts if you have the model number and part number. Keep any manuals or parts lists that come with an appliance that may contain parts numbers, ordering, or service instructions. Every number on the appliance may be important, so in correspondence, cite them all. The biggest problem in locating appliance parts is that there may be many different models, each with a different part. If you can establish the numerical identity of the part you need, you have a pretty good chance of getting it.

Rewiring a lamp

ALWAYS UNPLUG A LAMP BEFORE WORKING ON IT. Normally, only two things can go wrong with an ordinary lamp: either the switch wears out, or the cord and plug need replacing. Both are easy repair jobs. The switch is either in the light bulb receptacle, as in the lamp pictured, or it is a separate unit in the base of the lamp. The separate base switch is held in place by a single ring nut, which you can reach through the bottom of the base. Simply remove the nut, lift out the switch, and disconnect it. Install the new switch by connecting it to the same wires you took the old switch from, and tighten the ring nut. If your lamp has a switch receptacle, as shown here, begin by removing the top part of the receptacle. A pressure point on the receptacle, often indicated by the word "press," is the key to removal. Press this point with your thumb, or insert a screwdriver between the top and the base, and at the same time, pull up on the top.

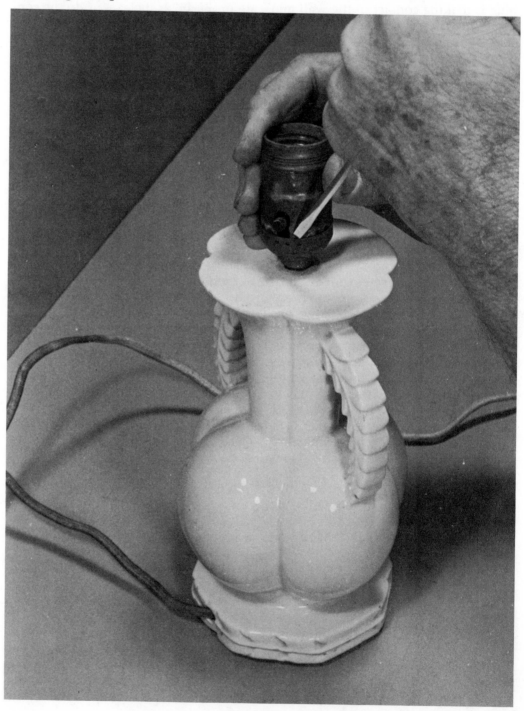

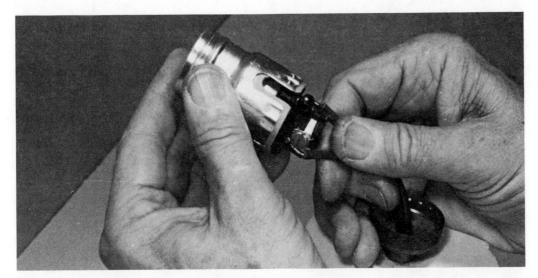

When the top part of the receptacle is separated from the bottom, the interior part of the receptacle and the wire connections are exposed. Use a screwdriver to loosen the contact screws, then remove the wires.

Sometimes fishing a new wire through a lamp can be tricky. One way to avoid problems is to attach a string to the old wire before pulling it out of the lamp. With the string attached, pull the wire through. Remove the old wire from the string, and tie the new wire to it. When you pull the string back through the lamp, the new wire follows. (You won't need this trick every time, but it is handy to know.)

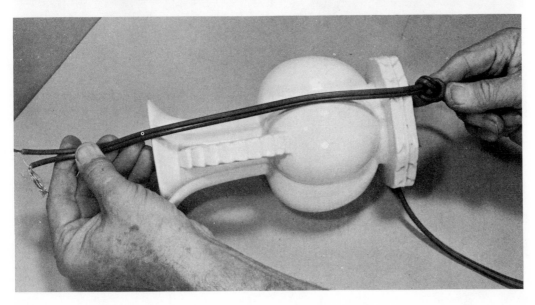

If someone pulls on the lamp cord, it might pull the electrical connections in the lamp loose. To prevent this, tie a knot in the cord, as shown. The knot is inside the base when the wire is in place, and prevents any pulling pressure on the electrical connections.

Twist the strands of the new wires together, and connect each wire to a screw on the new socket base by wrapping the wire around each screw post from left to right. As the screw is turned, the wire is tightened. When you have made these connections, pull the wire from the bottom of the lamp base until the receptacle is seated snugly; then slip the cover over the base, and press it into place. Cement a new felt pad onto the lamp base, and install a new plug on the cord.

Caring for an iron

An electric iron is a simple and well-constructed piece of household equipment. Electrically, about the only repair you'll ever have to make is to replace the power cord. Irons require a special cord insulated with asbestos. You can buy the cord complete with plug and wires formed into loops and ready to connect to the iron. You will find an access plate near the back of the iron, held in place by a screw. Remove the screw, and take the plate off to see how the power cord connects to the iron. Remove the two screws holding the power cord wires. Next, take off the two small fiber glass sleeves that protect the cord wires, and set them aside. (You will reinstall them later.) Pull the cord out a few inches to expose a metal washer clamped to it. The washer prevents pulling pressure on the electrical connections. Use pliers to remove this washer, and put it aside for reinstallation.

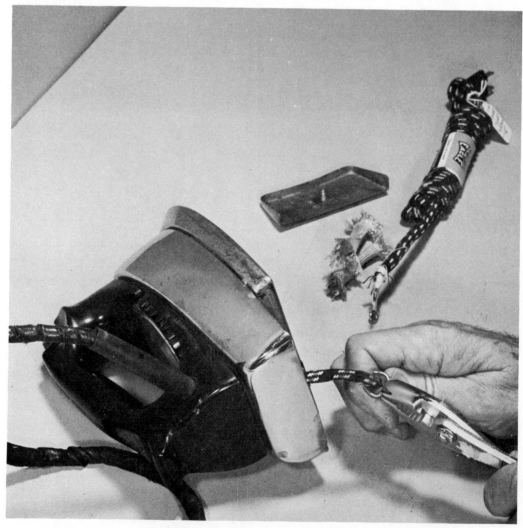

Attach a string to the old cord before pulling it out completely. The string makes it easy to pull the new cord back through the protective housing.

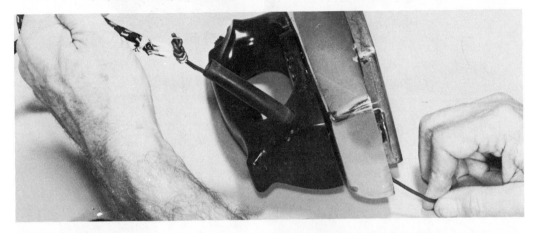

Tie the new cord to the string, and pull it back through the iron.

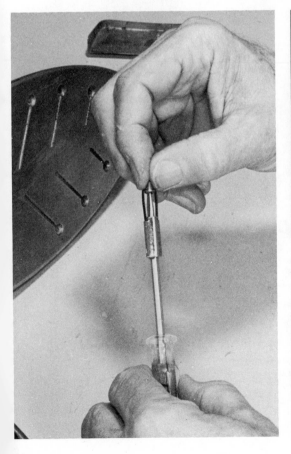

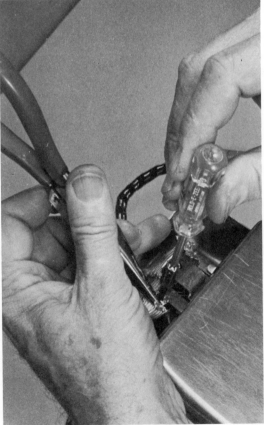

Far left:
Replace the screws that connect the cord wires; use a screwdriver with spring-clip fingers to hold the screw firmly while you turn it.

Left:
To make the new power cord connection, slip the fiber-glass sleeves onto the power cord wires, and hold the wire in place with needlenose pliers while you insert and tighten each screw. Reinstall the metal washer on the power cord, using pliers, and replace the cover plate.

Caring for a toaster

Right:
NEVER WORK ON A TOASTER WHEN IT IS PLUGGED IN. If toast gets stuck in the toaster, DON'T try to dig it out with a knife or fork, especially when the toaster is plugged in. You may get a serious shock and do serious damage to the heating elements. Unplug the toaster, then carefully work out the stuck item, being sure you don't contact heating elements. These consist of fine wires that are easily broken. Clean out the crumbs which accumulate in the toaster tray. The tray is a trap door which is easily opened.

Far right:
Not all of the crumbs fall into the tray. Some collect on the working parts, causing your toaster to work improperly. Use a soft brush, but don't brush vigorously, or you may damage parts.

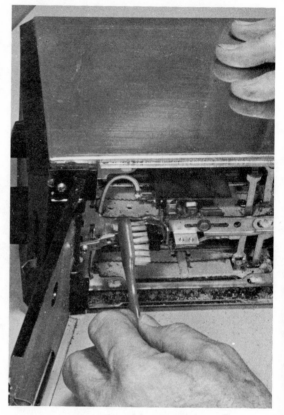

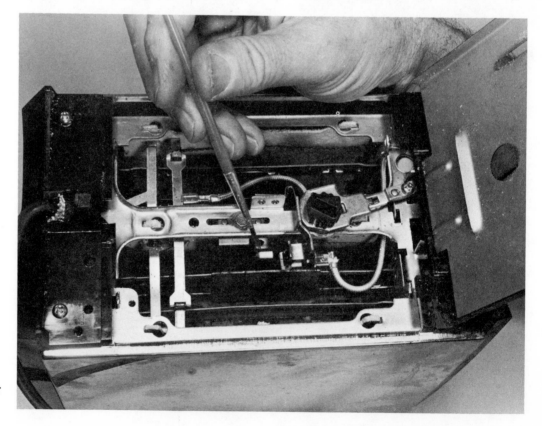

The heart of your toaster's controls is a small bimetal switch, which is very delicate and should be cleaned carefully with a small, artist's brush. One crumb lodged in this switch can put your toaster out of commission.

Caring for a can opener

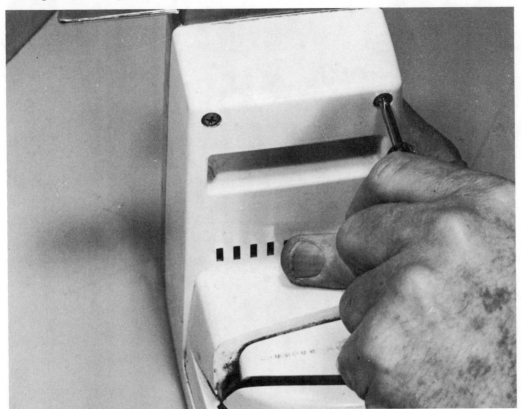

Electric can openers are usually trouble free. The only problems you are likely to encounter are the need to replace the power cord and to clean the contact points on the main switch inside. UNPLUG THE UNIT before removing the outside shell.

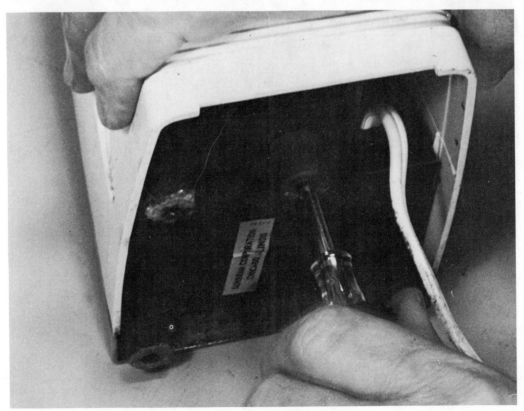

Sometimes the screws that hold an appliance together are easy to see and taking it apart is no problem. At other times these screws are cleverly hidden. On this can opener, one of the screws is inside a rubber foot. Another favorite hiding place is behind the metal identification plate; you must take the plate off to find the screw.

To replace the power cord
loosen the solderless
connectors, take off the old
cord, and use the same
connectors to connect the
new cord.

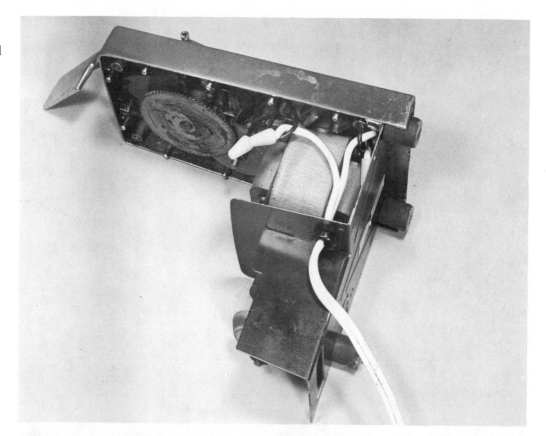

Every can opener model
has a slightly different type
of contact switch, but the
contact principle is always
the same: when you press
down on the operating
handle, two points inside
the can opener are forced
to make contact. The can
opener works as long as
this contact is made, but if
dirt or grease interfere, the
unit won't work. To clean
these contact points, slide a
piece of rough paper
between them a few times.
It acts like a very fine
sandpaper. After cleaning,
depress the outside lever,
and watch to see that the
two points make contact. If
they don't, you may have
to bend the movable arm
on which one of the points
is located. A slight bend is
usually all that is required
and can be done with
needlenose pliers.

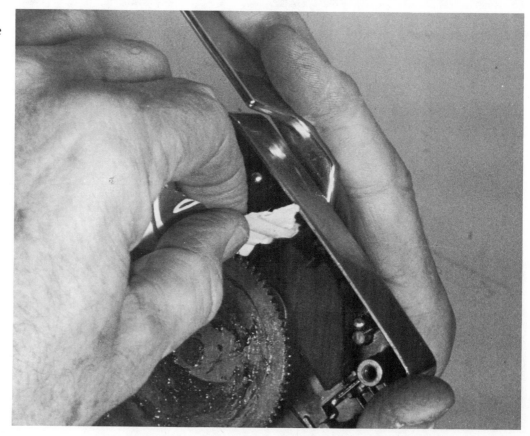

Caring for a coffee maker

If your coffee maker isn't working or isn't making good coffee, look for several causes. Begin by cleaning the percolator tube thoroughly. Very often deposits in the tube narrow it down so that too little water is pumped through it. This produces weak coffee and eventually stops the coffee-making action entirely. Boiling a mixture of water and baking soda in the pot will sweeten it and get rid of old coffee oils, or you can buy a commercial product to do the same thing. A strong vinegar solution also will help get rid of deposits in the percolator tube. The next place to look for a problem is inside the base of the pot. If the base of your coffee maker can be removed, you will find screws in the bottom. Some pots are made so that the base cannot be removed, these cannot be repaired.

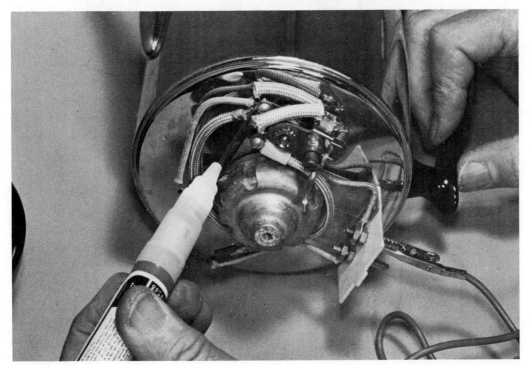

A possible problem is that the coffee pot may not be getting electrical current. Buy a simple circuit tester, which can be a help with all appliance and electrical work. The tester is battery powered and can be used when the appliance is unplugged. In this picture, the alligator clip of the tester is attached to one prong of the pot's plug-in unit. The probe of the tester is then touched to contact points in the circuit. A bulb in the tester handle lights to tell you when a circuit is closed so that current can pass through it. If the wire between the plug prong and the switch is broken, the circuit tester bulb will not light.

A coffee maker usually depends on one or more bimetal switches to turn its heating elements on and off and to control the temperature of the coffee. If these are burned or dirty, they won't work properly. A strip of paper, cut from a grocery bag, pulled back and forth between the contact points of the switches will clean them.

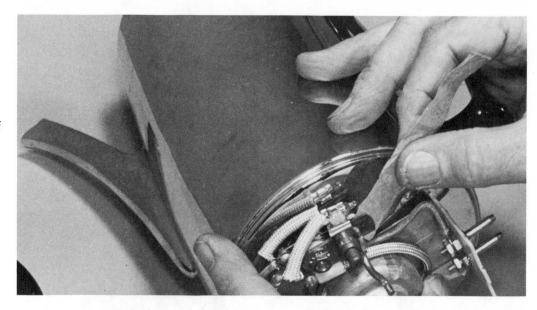

Caring for an electric mixer

Right:
Like other appliances in your kitchen, the electric mixer is fairly simple and consists of a motor controlled by a switch. Depending on the model you have, the switch may be constant speed, two- or three-speed, or adjustable over a wide range of speeds. Barring complicated motor problems, the only repairs you may have to make are cleaning the switch and replacing the power cord. The first task, *after unplugging the mixer*, is to take off the outer shell.

Far right:
Inside the shell, you can see where the power cord is connected to the motor. Replacing the power cord is simply a matter of removing the solderless connectors, disconnecting the old power cord, connecting the new wires, and replacing the new connectors.

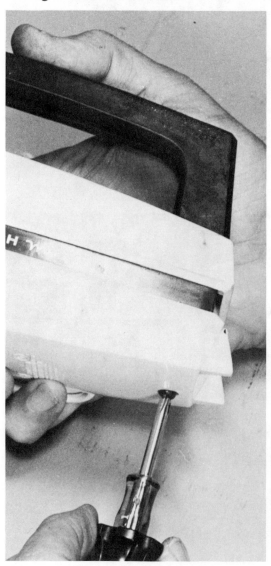

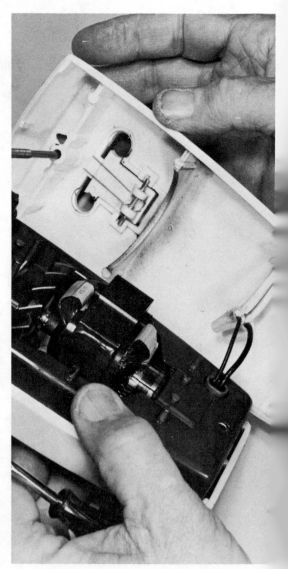

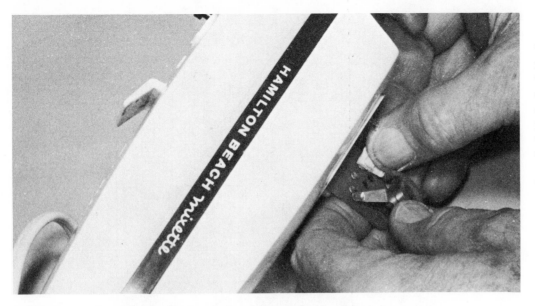

The switch elements in this mixer are located inside the handle. The switch consists of a movable arm and four copper contact points. Use a piece of coarse paper to clean any dirt or carbon from these points. If any part of the switch is broken, you can usually get replacement parts by writing to the manufacturer. Be sure to include all information — model number, year, etc.

Caring for a portable electric oven

There are two types of portable electric ovens: one type is similar in design to a toaster but is larger and has better controls; the other type is designed for use as a broiler.

The most common repair in either type oven is the installation of a new power cord. The first step, *with the unit unplugged,* is to gain access to the interior electrical connections. Every make and model has a different type of access. The end panels on this model must be removed by taking out two bolt-headed screws.

With the end panel off, you can see how the power cord is attached. Use a circuit tester to find out whether or not the problem is in the power cord. Attach the alligator clip to one prong of the plug, and touch the probe to the power cord contacts inside the unit. The light should come on when you touch one of the contacts. Repeat this test with the other prong. If the light doesn't come on, the power cord is faulty and should be replaced.

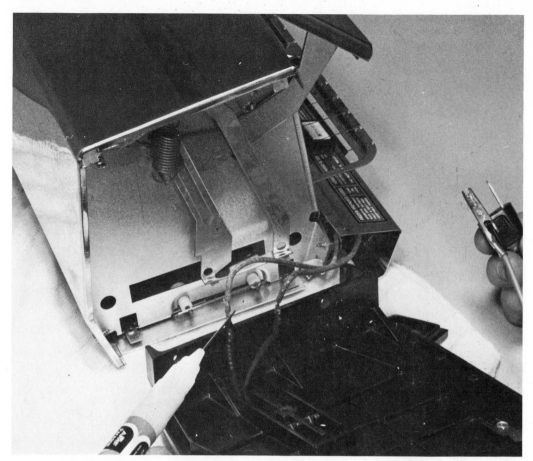

Caring for an electric frying pan

Electric frying pans are sturdy and not subject to many problems. The pans are of two types: the kind you can put into water and the kind you cannot. The type shown here, with the detachable heating element, can be totally submersed in water. The other type must be washed carefully so that no water gets into the electrical parts. If you should accidentally dunk a nonsubmersible pan, DON'T USE IT AGAIN UNTIL IT IS THOROUGHLY DRY. Take off the bottom plate, exposing the electrical parts, and use a fan or a hair dryer to blow warm air over the wet parts. Be sure they are bone dry before putting the pan away.

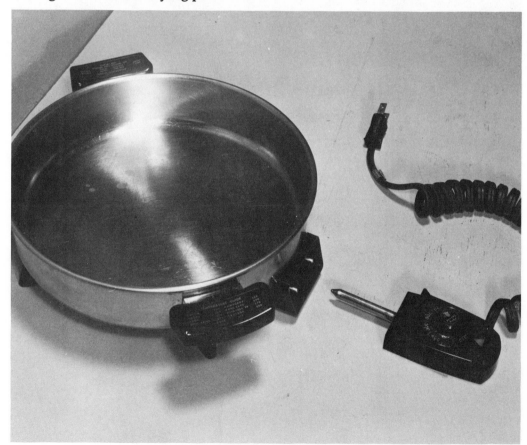

The doorbell system

The heart of your doorbell system is the transformer, shown here mounted on the junction box of a basement light. Locate your doorbell's transformer. (If your house has a basement, it will be in the ceiling of the basement.) The transformer reduces the 115-volt household current to the current required for your doorbell system. If you have a very old doorbell system, the transformer may be of the 6-volt type. If you have a more modern system, it is likely to be of the 16-volt type. All chime systems, for example, run on 16 volts. These transformers are not interchangeable. If you are installing a new system or updating an old one, start with a 16-volt transformer.

Doorbell systems are wired with bell wire, which you can buy in small rolls. Don't use bell wire for any but low voltage systems. Problems in the doorbell system usually involve the buttons, which wear out or get rusty. You can test a button by removing the wires from it and touching the two wires together. If the bell rings, you know the problem is in the button, and it should be replaced. Transformers seldom need replacement. The bell or chime units are sometimes a trouble source. After checking the buttons out, examine the chime unit for loose wires and for accumulations of dirt and grease (especially if the chime unit is located in the kitchen). If dirt or lack of lubrication binds the movement of the plunger, it won't strike the chime tube, even though the rest of the system is working properly. After cleaning the plunger movement, lubricate the plunger by spraying it with powdered graphite; don't use oil.

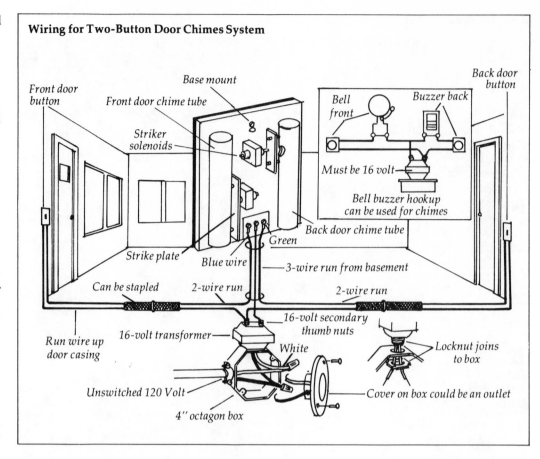

Wiring for Two-Button Door Chimes System

Front door button

Base mount

Front door chime tube

Striker solenoids

Strike plate

Blue wire

Can be stapled

2-wire run

Run wire up door casing

16-volt transformer

Unswitched 120 Volt

4″ octagon box

Back door button

Bell front

Buzzer back

Must be 16 volt

Bell buzzer hookup can be used for chimes

Back door chime tube

Green

3-wire run from basement

2-wire run

16-volt secondary thumb nuts

White

Locknut joins to box

Cover on box could be an outlet

Index